Where Two or Three are Gathered

Themed Resources for Group Worship

Lezley J. Stewart

SAINT ANDREW PRESS
Edinburgh

First published in 2014 by
SAINT ANDREW PRESS
121 George Street
Edinburgh EH2 4YN

It is the publisher's policy to only use papers that are natural and
recyclable and that have been manufactured from timber grown
in renewable, properly managed forests. All of the manufacturing
processes of the papers are expected to conform to the environmental
regulations of the country of origin.

Typeset by Regent Typesetting, London

Printed and bound in the United Kingdom by
CPI Group (UK) Ltd

Contents

Introduction

There are many occasions when small groups worship together, and the Bible reminds us that where two or three are gathered, God is there (Matthew 18:20).

This book is intended to resource such worship, and allow meaningful reflection to take place. The text provides ready-made services, or resources to be used as part of church meetings or group gatherings.

Each element of the text can be used in the sequence offered or easily combined with other elements. The flexible format is designed to support readers who are looking for ready-made material or for something that they can adapt to their own situation.

The resources are accessible to all, and do not require an ordained person to lead. They are written in a way that has not been personalised by the author, so that they can be used straight from the page to aid and encourage worship in any situation. They can also be shared among the group.

Through the prayers and reflections, people are encouraged to worship together, joining their voices in prayer, and reflecting on God's word and how it engages with their life. There are perhaps more questions asked than answers given, which reflects the life of faith.

May you find blessing in leading the worship of God.

Notes on using these resources

This book is in three parts:

Part 1: Prayer Liturgies

Twelve Prayer Liturgies are provided. Each is based on a key theme in our lives and worship. Within each of the Prayer Liturgies, it is suggested that a Biblical Reflection is used and Part 2 of the book provides four suggested Biblical readings per theme and four reflections to choose from, depending on the occasion.

Each of the prayer liturgies can be used four times with the accompanying reflections – or you can prepare your own reflection. Those gathered to worship are encouraged to join the prayer responses at the beginning and end, and these are provided for photocopying at the end of the book. Within the liturgies, there is an opportunity to include items of praise as appropriate to your group.

Creative centre

There is a suggestion for each liturgy of an item which can be placed in the sight of the worship group. You may wish to use this suggestion to help focus people's thoughts.

Part 2: Biblical Reflections

Based on each of the 12 prayer liturgies, there are four suggested Biblical readings with accompanying reflections – in total, 48 reflections.

At the appropriate part in the time of worship, the Biblical passage should be read, followed by the written reflection. Following that, there is an opportunity to guide people in a time of reflection, which can be in silence or with background music, to consider the areas highlighted in 'Time to Reflect'.

Part 3: Group Prayer Responses

These are the prayer responses shown in Part 1 and are provided here for the group to use. They have been designed to ensure ease of photocopying. Each one (of twelve) can be circulated or displayed as suits the group best or they can be printed on an A5 card with the explanatory notes provided on the opposite side as appropriate.

PRAYER LITURGIES

TIMING

DRAWING NEAR

Time never stands still
But our God is eternal

Yesterday, today and tomorrow
God is unchanging

Here and now, in this precious time
May we meet with God

PRAISE

Here a hymn or psalm may be read or sung

APPROACH

God of each day and night, as we experience the sun's setting and rising, marking a day now passed and announcing the arrival of another, we know you are the God of time and eternity.

We praise you that in each moment of each day, recognised and unrecognised, you are in our midst.

For the gift of your presence, we bless you.
For the wonder of your love, we thank you.
For the promise of eternity, we worship you.

As time passes, sometimes too quickly and other times too slowly – a moving hand on an ever-changing clock – we are conscious that time never stands still, and you, our God, are always active.

Through the activities of our lives we have sought to serve you in different ways, and yet we know the times we have let you and ourselves down. In a moment of quietness, we take time to reflect on our faults and failings – taking the time to ask for your forgiveness and the chance to begin again ...

Silence

Lord, in this time – your time – remind us again of your unfailing presence and your gifts, graciously given for all time and eternity. Amen

THE WORD

Biblical reading, homily and time for reflection

PRAYING FOR OTHERS

Eternal God, we often hear people say that 'time is a great healer', but we believe that you are a healing God, and so we take the time to bring you our prayerful concerns, trusting in your timing to bring forth hope and wholeness.

We give thanks for this time where we can worship you freely and pray for those under threat of violence or living under oppression, that a time may come when peace will reign.

Lord, in your mercy, **Hear our prayer**

We pray for those for whom the years have not been kind; where there has been loss of hopes and dreams, where love has been lost, where grief has been felt and pain has become an unwelcome companion.

Lord, in your mercy, **Hear our prayer**

We pray for all who have past regrets and who long for freedom through forgiveness. We remember all who are anxious and fearful for the future, and all for whom this time is difficult.

Lord, in your mercy, **Hear our prayer**

In a time of stillness we bring our personal prayers to God, who has promised to hear our concerns ...

Silence

Lord of eternity, all time is in your hands. Let us place our trust in you – today, tomorrow and always. Amen

PRAISE

Here a hymn or psalm may be read or sung

CLOSING RESPONSES

All time is in God's hands
Lord, we have met with you this day/night

Into your hands we commit our lives
Bless us, O Lord God of life

Send us out in your name
Go with us now, we pray

BLESSING

May God bless, preserve and keep us, now and for evermore. Amen

UNITY

CREATIVE CENTRE –
A COMPLETED JIGSAW

DRAWING NEAR

Where two or three are gathered
God is there

As we gather this day/night
God is here

Here and now and always
God is with us

PRAISE

Here a hymn or psalm may be read or sung

APPROACH

Great God, you have revealed yourself in the patterns of
this earth. As the many colours of the spectrum become one
rainbow, so we see your symbol of promise, uniting us as one
people. May we be a living sign of your promise.

In the love revealed in your Son, and demonstrated shockingly
on a cross, we hear your call to be your people – that the earth
and all its people might know you as Lord. May we be a people
united in faith.

In challenging teaching and living, the life of your Son shakes
our complacency and comfort, to view the life of the world in a
new way. May we respond to your truth and to your way.
In perfect love, revealed in Christ, we see the inconsistencies of
our lives, where pride and jealousy, fear and indifference have
broken the bonds which should bind us as one. Forgive our
faults and make us one in your love, we pray.

As each new day begins with no mistakes in it, may we receive
your forgiveness in our hearts, and hear your call afresh in our
souls. Unite us in purpose and passionate living, for the Christ
who is our Lord. Amen

THE WORD

Biblical reading, homily and time for reflection

PRAYING FOR OTHERS

In a world where all the pieces do not seem to fit together, we
come to you, our God, who is able to make all things new.

Where there is division in the body of Christ;
in churches and communities;
in denominations and institutions,
may your call be heard clearly and simply again – 'follow me'.

We pray, O Lord, for our broken earth;
for lands that are parched and people who hunger and thirst;
for places where people stand divided, forgetting how much they
share in common;
for those who use words to spread hate and fear and ignore your
message of love and peace.

We think of divided families, of failed relationships and broken
promises. We pray for your healing to tie together common
threads, that hope may be created again. Wherever there is pain
and division, bring your love.

In our own lives, we know those in special need of your touch. We name them before you now …

Silence

O God, in you we live and move and have our being. Unite us in your love, that our lives become a sign of promise to all whom we serve in your name. Amen

PRAISE

Here a hymn or psalm may be read or sung

CLOSING RESPONSES

Make us one, Lord, in your love
Make us one, Lord, in your name

May your life be known in our lives
May your love shine through us

BLESSING

May the blessing of the one, and the blessing of the three, entwine together thee and me. Amen

PROVIDENCE

CREATIVE CENTRE – A MAP

DRAWING NEAR

In the journey of life
God makes known a path

Through rough and smooth, twist and turn
God is our guiding strength

Through the adventure that is faith
Our trust is in God

PRAISE

Here a hymn or psalm may be read or sung

APPROACH

As a path through the countryside is only created by those who have chosen to walk the same way, we come together to seek your way for our lives, O Lord.

We draw near to you, the God of life, who from the beginning of time have shown through great faithfulness a desire to lead and guide your people.

Your ways, O Lord, are not our ways, and we are conscious of the many choices given to us in life, and the different decisions we make. We thank you for the freedom to choose, but confess how often we choose our own ways over yours, wanting to benefit ourselves rather than the life of the world.

Where we have ignored you – make forgiveness your gift.

Where we have disobeyed you – set our feet on firm ground again.

Where we have disowned you – call our name and let us hear your voice.

You, O God, have guided your people through every time and every place, and have shown us that faith is a journey. May we in this generation continue that journey, inspired and challenged by those who have gone before us. Speak to us now, as you have spoken in the past, and let us know your will for our lives. Amen

THE WORD

Biblical reading, homily and time for reflection

PRAYING FOR OTHERS

Living Lord, not a day goes by where we do not have to make decisions. Each day brings its challenges and confrontations and the choice to live for you.

We pray, O Lord, for all facing decisions at this time – whether at home, or work; for all making choices that affect the lives of those around them. Show your way, O God.

We bring our prayers for all who hold responsibility through government and agency; for all who have the ability to make an impact for good or bad. Make your wisdom known, O God.

We pray for all who have made bad choices in the past and live with bitterness and regret. Renew and refresh what is old and tired, we pray.

We bring our prayers for ourselves and the decisions we have to make each day. Lord, help us know your hand leading and guiding us, yet never compelling us.

In a moment of stillness we bring to mind the people and situations that need your inspiration at this time ...

Silence

God of life, you have blessed us and all your people. May we go forward in faith, knowing your plans for us are for a future blessed in you. Amen

PRAISE

Here a hymn or psalm may be read or sung

CLOSING RESPONSES

Our God has shown us the Way
Let us go forward in faith

Our God has revealed to us the Truth
Let us live in truth each day

Our God has blessed us with Life
Let us live our lives for God

BLESSING

May God grant his blessing to each and to all, both now and for evermore. Amen

CREATION

CREATIVE CENTRE – LEAVES/FLOWERS

DRAWING NEAR

Through sunshine, cloud and rain
God blesses the earth

Amid earth's myriad of colours
God's glory is seen

As part of God's creation
We know our Creator is near

PRAISE

Here a hymn or psalm may be read or sung

APPROACH

In the splendour of a sunrise, in the beauty of a sunset;
in the roar of thunder or a whispering through the trees;
through the glory of the changing seasons;
you, O God, are revealed in majesty.

We praise you, O God, for the beauty of the earth, and for
the gift of the world to be our home. We give thanks for the
wondrous difference you created in humanity, and the complex
patterns by which life is sustained.

You call us, Lord, to care for the world and be stewards of all we share. We are conscious, Lord, and we therefore confess our wastefulness and our wantonness in abusing your creation. We recognise we enjoy more than our fair share of the abundance of the earth, and while we thrive, others suffer. We confess we often fail to see the repercussions of choices we make, and we forget who our neighbour is.

Lord, forgive us we pray, and challenge us again to care for all you have created. May our eyes never be closed to the beauty that surrounds us, our ears never be closed to the cries of those who need us, and our hearts always be open to the Spirit who leads us.

Creative God, make us a new creation, we pray. Amen

THE WORD

Biblical reading, homily and time for reflection

PRAYING FOR OTHERS

Living Spirit, you are moving and breathing in the world we enjoy and share. We thank you for your presence with us and in us, inspiring our lives and shaping our living. You call us to care for the earth and all its people, and we bring our prayers to you now in faith.

For the parts of the earth burdened by drought, and the places overwhelmed by rains we pray. Lord, in your wisdom, guide your people to work with your creation rather than against it.

Where there is pollution and contamination heal the broken earth and the practices which poison. Inspire careful use of chemicals and creative use of crops that the earth may yield for its people.

We pray for all that is threatened by climate change and ask for preservation and protection to conserve all that is precious. Make us value difference and diversity and play our own part.

We pray for a just and equal sharing; for generosity between nations and for a world of plenty to be a world that provides for all people.

Lord, we are your people. Make known your ways and let the earth tell again of your glory. In Jesus' name. Amen

PRAISE

Here a hymn or psalm may be read or sung

CLOSING RESPONSES

From the earth we came
We belong to God

To the earth we will return
We belong to God

Let us go to care for the earth and its people
For we belong to God

BLESSING

May God add his blessing to his creation, through us, his creation. In Christ's name. Amen

GROWTH

CREATIVE CENTRE – A PLANT

DRAWING NEAR

As new buds burst forth in Springtime
May our love for God blossom

Where beauty and colour enrich the earth
May our lives be a fragrant offering

As a seed sown awaits its potential
May we grow each day in God

PRAISE

Here a hymn or psalm may be read or sung

APPROACH

Lord, you have sown the seeds of faith in our hearts and minds
and you draw us close to you in this time together. Each of us
comes with our different thoughts and experiences and you, O
Lord, know where we are in the journey of faith and life. Living
God, walk with us, we pray.

We give thanks, O God, for your call, heard in our lives, and for
the different ways you ask us to respond. We thank you for all
who encourage us on the journey and for your Spirit who has
given and inspires our gifts. Help us, gracious God, to grow in
our lives of service and grow ever closer to you.

Life-giving Spirit, you are always with us to encourage and equip, yet we often rely only on our own strength. When we are guilty of hiding our talents, when we are wishful of a quiet and unchallenging life, forgive us and renew your call in our lives. Give us confidence and courage, we pray, to live our lives for you.

Loving Spirit, grow in our hearts and minds your peace and truth, that growing in faith all glory be given to God alone. Amen

THE WORD

Biblical reading, homily and time for reflection

PRAYING FOR OTHERS

You, O God, bless us with the gifts of life to nourish and sustain us. As we have known your blessing and your love growing in our hearts, we pray for your blessing upon your people.

We pray for all who are growing in faith at this time – asking questions and seeking and searching. May you be for them, a path to follow.

We pray for all who have grown stale in their faith, no longer hearing your voice and your challenge. Lord, speak again to these hearts that they might hear your call afresh and respond with new vigour and faith.

We pray for all whose lives are stunted by lack of care and compassion – for the ignored, the neglected – the children orphaned and unsupported. We remember your love is as a parent's love for a child. Make that love known, we ask.

We pray for all who do not have the opportunities to grow in knowledge and potential – for all deprived of education and employment – all whose nurture is hampered by poverty and disease. May your love inspire change and new chances.

Grow in our hearts and minds, Lord, the compassion you have for your people. Make our lives work for you and lead us on in your name, we pray. Amen

PRAISE

Here a hymn or psalm may be read or sung

CLOSING RESPONSES

Rooted in God
Let us go forward in faith

Nourished in the Lord
Let us go in his strength

Fed by his Word
Let us live to his glory

BLESSING

May the blessing of God guard, support and sustain us, each and every day. Amen

SERVICE

DRAWING NEAR

Call to us now, Lord
That we may hear your voice

Come to us now, Lord
That we might seek your way

Meet with us now, Lord
That we might praise your name

PRAISE

Here a hymn or psalm may be read or sung

APPROACH

He came to earth, not to be served, and so we come to Christ, who has called to us. We bless you, Lord Jesus Christ, that you have made yourself one with us, and have experienced and shared our lives with us.

Servant King, may your life be reflected in ours – your love, your service and your devotion. May your words become our words, your thoughts become our thoughts, and your actions become our actions.

O Christ, who befriended the poor and oppressed, the women and the outcast, we confess that our lives often exclude rather than include. We are conscious of our prejudice and preferences, and the way we can make people feel unwelcome and unwanted. Challenge us and change us, Lord, we pray, and forgive our failings. Help us to be changed that we do not go on making the same mistakes again and again, but by your Spirit equip us for service.

Lord Jesus Christ, you led by example, so may we be inspired to become your hands and feet working in the world today, serving your people, and sharing your message of love and transformation.

Create in us a new heart, O Lord, and renew a right spirit within us. Amen

THE WORD

Biblical reading, homily and time for reflection

PRAYING FOR OTHERS

The love of God is shown in love that gets its hands dirty and meets people where they are. Lord, let that love be shown in us.

As we seek to serve you, we come to pray for your people – for all with whom we share this life, this world, and the adventure of faith.

Bring blessing we pray to all who devote their lives to serving others – those in the caring professions, those in the service industry who get so little credit, but on whom society depends.

We pray for all who work for charities and development agencies, who keep the needs of others always in mind. Lord, may your love be known in the work they do, and in the lives changed and transformed as a result.

We pray for those who need to be cared for – the lonely and distressed, the ill and the anxious, the bereaved and the dying. Lord, as you served, teach us to serve. Let your life be known in ours.

Together with these prayers we add those resting in our own hearts and minds in a time of quiet ...

Silence

Inspired by your life of service, Lord, let us live our lives for you. Amen

PRAISE

Here a hymn or psalm may be read or sung

CLOSING RESPONSES

Our God calls us to serve
May we not seek to be served

Through Christ we see the way
May we follow in faith

As Jesus pointed to the Father
Let all glory be to God alone

BLESSING

May the blessing of the God of Life, the Christ of Love and the Spirit of Peace be with us all. Amen

JUSTICE

DRAWING NEAR

The Lord is just and merciful
His compassion is unending

He is perfect beyond compare
His faithfulness is never exhausted

He is higher than the heavens, yet present with us now
Let us draw near to God

PRAISE

Here a hymn or psalm may be read or sung

APPROACH

Above our highest thoughts, beyond our wildest dreams –
you are our God.

Greater than our understanding, closer than our every breath –
you draw near, O God.

We worship and praise you for your unending love and justice,
which has been displayed and demonstrated throughout
generations.

Gracious God, for your high standards, for your challenging call, for your desire to let justice and mercy reign, we bring our praise.

You, O Lord, have shown us perfection in Jesus Christ your Son. In him we see your life – in him we know your love – through him we hear your call. Let us be your faithful followers we pray.

For our inability to see with your eyes, forgive us, O God. For our failure to hear your voice among many competing voices, forgive us, O God. For our desire to choose the easier way, forgive us, O God.

Lord, your way is narrow. Renew and restore us to walk with you, bringing your peace and justice to the earth. Amen

THE WORD

Biblical reading, homily and time for reflection

PRAYING FOR OTHERS

Gracious God, we acknowledge that we live in a world where the scales of justice are unbalanced. Through the world's voices we hear your cry to bring your good news to troubled hearts. Hear our prayer, we ask.

We bring our prayers for those who are imprisoned. For all who are deprived of their freedom, whether through crime or oppression, we ask for your justice to reign.

We pray for all who suffer at the hands of others, directly or indirectly. We pray for ethical trading and governments who care for the underprivileged. We pray that you would convict your people of the part we all play in allowing injustice in our church, our communities and our world.

We pray for all who uphold the civil law, and all who work for a better society. We pray for all trying to follow your Law, O Lord, and ask for your guiding wisdom.

Lord, your ways are not our ways, but we recommit ourselves to your path – let justice and mercy flow, we pray. Amen

PRAISE

Here a hymn or psalm may be read or sung

CLOSING RESPONSES

A blameless life, given for us
Let your life be lived in ours

A wondrous love, gifted to us
Let your love be seen in us

A life of justice, lived in truth
Let justice reign in our hearts

BLESSING

May grace, mercy and peace from God the Father, Spirit and Son guide our lives and our living, this and every day. Amen

LOVE

DRAWING NEAR

Love is greater than all things
Our God is love

His love is arms stretched out upon a cross
Our God is love

Such love calls us to humble service
Let us love God with heart, mind, soul and strength

PRAISE

Here a hymn or psalm may be read or sung

APPROACH

Love is where God is, and so we gather in your love, O Lord.
We thank you for your love made known in the life, death and
resurrection of your Son – a love that is eternal and offered
freely.

Let us meet in your love, Lord, and know you are close. Let us
hear your promise to be always with us, and know it to be true.
Let us offer our lives to you again, that you may accept us as we
are and inspire us in your service.

Your love, O God, is the love that calls ordinary people to do extraordinary things. In the shadow of your Son we feel truly blessed to be called by you, but sense our inadequacies to carry out the task.

As with the first disciples, forgive our lack of faith and confidence, and remind us all things are possible with you. Make us aware of your Spirit, guiding us in your love, that we might be known as your disciples today.

Bless us in our worship and in our common life together, that we may know we are gathered together in your love. Amen

THE WORD

Biblical reading, homily and time for reflection

PRAYING FOR OTHERS

Your love, O God, reaches to the heavens, and yet surrounds our earthly life. We bless you for your constant love and guidance.

We bring our prayers for a hurting world where your love needs to be made known. Make us instruments of your peace and channels of your love, we pray.

We pray for our Christian brothers and sisters throughout the world, both near and far away – may we be bound together in your love. Where there are differences, let us be healed by your love.

We pray for all who feel unloved and unwanted. We remember the lonely, those separated by distance or trial from loved ones, those suffering exclusion from society through unemployment, homelessness or illness.

We bring our prayers for those for whom love has been lost – where a child has broken all ties, where a relationship has broken down, and where a loved one has died. As you open your arms to receive your children, bring healing to troubled hearts, we pray.

We bring our prayers for those known personally to us, in need of your love ...

Silence

God of love, make us more loving, day by day. Amen

PRAISE

Here a hymn or psalm may be read or sung

CLOSING RESPONSES

God is love
We go to live in the love of God

God is life
We go to live in fullness of life

God is living
We go to spread the good news

BLESSING

May Christ's blessing go before and behind us, and be known through us day by day. Amen

LIFE

> ## CREATIVE CENTRE –
> ## DIARY/WALL PLANNER

DRAWING NEAR

God calls us to new life in him
Every day is new with God

God calls us to life in all its fullness
May the Spirit fill our lives

Life in God is life everlasting
May our lives be filled with praise

PRAISE

Here a hymn or psalm may be read or sung

APPROACH

Yours is the gift of life, O God, for you have knitted us together and woven our lives into yours; for this we praise and thank you.

We stand amazed to know that your knowledge of us is unsurpassed, and that you are before and behind us, above and below us, surrounding us with your love and care.

We worship you, living Lord, for blessing our lives each day through word and action and experience, and making each day new with you.

Lord Jesus, our lives are but a poor shadow of what you call us to be. You ask us to reflect your life in our lives and we are sorry for how we let you down. When we are selfish and uncaring, critical and unhelpful, we not only do a disservice to ourselves, but more importantly to you. Lord, forgive us, and transform us by your Spirit day by day.

Lord, let us live for you, as you lived, died and rose again to bring us life eternal. Amen

THE WORD

Biblical reading, homily and time for reflection

PRAYING FOR OTHERS

The journey of life is full of many surprises, but in all things you, the God of life, are with us.

We bring our prayers for each other, that in our living, and in our loving, we may know your blessing both near and true.

We pray for those beginning their lives; those yet unborn, those newly born, and for children growing each day. May they know they are all children of God.

We pray for all struggling in life – through trials and tribulations, through anxiety and depression, through illness and pain. Lord, bring your healing touch.

We pray for all nearing the end of life, and all who care for them. May there be freedom from fear, and an ability to appreciate all that life has given.

We bring to mind all who share our lives and who are in particular need at this time – hear our prayers for them now ...

Silence

Living God, continue the journey of life with us, and help us to trust in your promise never to leave nor forsake us. Amen

PRAISE

Here a hymn or psalm may be read or sung

CLOSING RESPONSES

Hope is a gift from God
Let us go with hope in our hearts

Peace is a gift from God
Let us share the peace of Christ

Joy is a gift from God
Let the joy of Christ fill our lives

BLESSING

May the blessing of God be with us, and with all God's people, now and always. Amen

KINGDOM

DRAWING NEAR

Your kingdom come, Lord
Your will be done

Let your kingdom be established
Let it be established in me

Your kingdom come, Lord
Let it begin with me

PRAISE

Here a hymn or psalm may be read or sung

APPROACH

Great God, you came to establish your kingdom, in and through your people. By the sending of your Son, you have revealed to us your ways, and have asked us to make your kingdom come.

We praise you for revealing your love and justice, your mercy and peace, and we stand in awe that you would make us partners in your work. What have we to offer, O Lord our God?

And yet in Christ we see how he taught and talked about your kingdom in ordinary, everyday ways. Through stories of seeds and sons, through images of light and love, help us, Lord, to grasp a vision of your kingdom.

Lord Jesus Christ, when our hearts are closed to your presence
– forgive us. When our minds are doubtful of your power –
transform us. When our souls are troubled by your message
– teach us.

We commit ourselves, Lord, to your vision and to your
kingdom, praying for that kingdom to be established now. Come
among us, Lord, we pray. Amen

THE WORD

Biblical reading, homily and time for reflection

PRAYING FOR OTHERS

Thy kingdom come, Lord. Hear our prayers as we join our
hearts and minds together to bring you our prayers and cast our
burdens upon you.

We pray, Lord, for a deeper understanding of your life, a deeper
reverence for your purpose, and a deeper longing to serve you.

We pray for all who seek to follow you, but find the path
is hard. Where there are hurdles to overcome – both social,
political and economic – establish your ways in this world, Lord.

We pray for all who long to see your peace. Instil in those who
talk of war a desire for peace. Challenge all who use violence by
the power of words of peace. Transform all who would preach
lies to live in your truth.

We pray for all who long to be reunited with loved ones in your
eternal kingdom. Wherever there is grief and pain, may your
light overcome the darkness.

We pray that you would establish your rule in our daily lives.
Search our hearts and find us not wanting, and then lead us in
your everlasting ways. Amen

PRAISE

Here a hymn or psalm may be read or sung

CLOSING RESPONSES

The kingdom of God is here
It is here in me

The kingdom of God is now
Let it live in me

Your will be done, living God
On earth as it is in heaven. Amen

BLESSING

May God bless us as we walk forward in faith, living in his truth, and sharing in his work. Amen

CHALLENGE

> CREATIVE CENTRE – A PUZZLE

DRAWING NEAR

From the security of our lives
We come to the sanctuary of God

Amid the world's noises and demands
We come to the peace of God

As we gather together in Christ's name
God, meet us here, we pray

PRAISE

Here a hymn or psalm may be read or sung

APPROACH

Each day and night, O God, we are challenged to display your love in our lives. As we meet together to bring our worship to you, may we hear that challenge again.

We give thanks for the variety of daily life, the people and the places that fill our days, and for the everyday opportunities to live lives that speak of you.

As Jesus revealed the character of you, our God, help us, we pray, to reflect the life of Jesus and not just some pale imitation. When we feel we are tempted to follow our own wisdom –

convince us of your truth. When we look to follow our own desires – remind us of your everlasting love. When we are driven to distraction – focus our eyes on you.

Forgive us, Lord, when we fail you and others by neglecting your call upon our lives. Reach out and embrace us, we pray, knowing that safe in your arms we are strengthened and equipped for the journey and adventure of faith.

Praise be to you, our gracious God. Amen

THE WORD

Biblical reading, homily and time for reflection

PRAYING FOR OTHERS

Living God, you are everywhere and at all times present. We thank you for blessing us with your Spirit. May your Spirit be in our hearts and minds this day, challenging us in our prayers and petitions to look beyond ourselves.

We pray to you, O God of truth, that amid the apparent wisdom of the world, your truth might reign supreme. Help us to follow your commandments, new and old, established for the blessing of the world.

We bring our prayers for all facing an upward struggle. Where there is tension, bring release. Where there is longing, bring fulfilment. Where there is pain, bring respite. Where there is potential, bring fruition.

In the twists and turns of life may all your people know your guiding hand, and hear our prayers for all the concerns resting in our hearts at this time ...

Silence

Each day is yours, Lord. Set us free from our worldly constraints that we might live confidently for you. Let your Spirit live in us and through us to your glory alone. Amen

PRAISE

Here a hymn or psalm may be read or sung

CLOSING RESPONSES

God goes before us
To show us the way

God goes behind us
Let us not stray

God goes with us
Bless us, we pray

BLESSING

May God grant his blessing to us as we go forward, keeping alive the faith, day by day. Amen

LIGHT

DRAWING NEAR

Out of the darkness and the void
Your light began to shine

Into the dark places of our lives
Shine your light, Lord

Into the dark corners of this world
Let us shine for you

PRAISE

Here a hymn or psalm may be read or sung

APPROACH

As light slowly filters into our lives each morning, awaking us
from sleep, so let the light of your presence filter into our lives as
we bring you our worship.

As we draw near to you, Lord, draw near to us, that we might
feel your Spirit light up our lives, bringing refreshment and
renewal.

We worship you, eternal God, for you have sent your Son into
the darkness of this world to be an eternal beacon of hope for
all who would trust and believe. May we be counted among the
faithful, we pray.

As you shed your light upon our lives, we are conscious of our many flaws and imperfections. What we would wish to hide, you bring into the light that never fades.

Take us as we are, O God, and purify us from all our sins. May our lives begin again to reflect your glory, drawing others to you like a moth is drawn to a flame.

Lord, shine your light amid our gathering this day. Be among and between us, uniting us in your love, your light and your life. Amen

THE WORD

Biblical reading, homily and time for reflection

PRAYING FOR OTHERS

You light up our lives, Living Lord, with your mercy and your grace. Let us never be found wanting. We bless you for your gifts to us and for the promise to hear our prayers.

In a dark world of trouble and tension, we pray for your light to illuminate all hatred and bitterness, that hearts may be transformed by your love.

We pray for all who live in darkness. For those who do not know your love or compassion, who find no love in a neighbour's heart, and who only know injustice and fear.

We pray for all who live with the darkness of depression and fear. For those with compulsive disorders and mental illness, for all where barriers are put up rather than broken down.

We pray for all who have known the darkness of death, losing a loved one and fearful of what the future holds. Bring your light out of the darkness.

Lord, shine a light into our hearts, that we might reflect your presence and be your people, loving and serving in the world. Amen

PRAISE

Here a hymn or psalm may be read or sung

CLOSING RESPONSES

Light has come into the world
And the darkness cannot hide it

Light has come in Christ our Lord
And the earth has seen his glory

Light has come into our lives
And we have been changed

BLESSING

May the light of Christ bring blessing to us and all God's people, both now and for evermore. Amen

BIBLICAL REFLECTIONS

TIMING

I

A time for everything

Ecclesiastes 3.1–14

Each of us will probably have a favourite time or season of the
year. Some will favour Spring over Summer, for the promise it
brings and the fresh cool breeze. Others will favour Autumn over
Winter for the crisp blue skies framed by the colourful, changing
leaves. There is a season for every activity under heaven.

And if you cast your mind back over the life you have so far
been blessed to enjoy, you might find that you have a favourite
time in your life, amid your years. Perhaps it was when you were
first employed, or those early years of marriage? Perhaps it was
when your first grandchild was born, or when your house became
a home? There is a time for everything in life.

Perhaps no truer words have come to us than these – 'there is
a time for everything', and to know in the midst of this time, that
in every time, God is there. Whether it be a time of sorrow or
joy, of love or hate, or tearing or mending, of speaking or silence.
Nothing can be added or taken away from these, for all time is in
God's hands.

So what of this time? Right here and right now? What time is
this for you? In your own heart, as you reflect on these words, you
will know what time you feel it to be. Perhaps a time of blessing,
or of transition, or of worry or of hope. And knowing that God
has set eternity in our hearts, but does not let us see his purpose

from beginning to end, we have to trust that this time is God's time, and he will make all things well.

There is no greater confirmation of the goodness of God, than to be able to look back over a difficult time in your life, and then at a distance, to be able to see the journey and all it has taught us for good. The Christian life does not shield us from pain and sadness; it does not promise a smooth path, but it assures us, time after time, that what God does will endure for ever, and that in every moment of every day, God is with us.

Time to reflect

- on what time this is in our lives
- on times of trial that we have suffered
- on times of blessing we have experienced
- on placing this time in God's hands, in faith.

TIMING

2

The gift of time

Luke 10.38–42

Entertaining people in your own home can be enjoyable, but it can also be a bit stressful! If you are the cook of the house, you probably want everything to be 'just so' for your guests arriving, and you hope all your skills in the kitchen will come to fruition. If you are not the cook of the house, you probably wonder what all the fuss is about, and think people should take you as they find you, and you don't quite understand why every room in the house has to be clean and tidy, when your guests will only be in one or two of them! Sound familiar?

Now what is the greater thing – to spend quality time with those you have invited and build on your friendship with them, or to wow them with cuisine and cleanliness? Hopefully you would agree the former is more important. It is the time that we spend with people, the gift of time and our attention, that people appreciate the most, and rightly so.

Consider then the story of Mary and Martha with their guest, Jesus. Yes, you can understand why Martha would be so distracted and annoyed at her sister, for there were things that were needing done! But equally, you can understand why Mary made the choice to simply enjoy being in the presence of Jesus, giving him her full and devoted attention.

No-one is suggesting that you might want to sit at the feet of your guests as Mary did, but we can learn from her example, that it is the sense of purpose and timing that is important. After all, this was to be her last quality time with her Lord, and Martha remained the poorer for fussing over the preparations. 'Only one thing is needed [and] Mary has chosen what is better,' says Jesus.

Every day in life is a gift, and we should recognise that it is God's gift to us, and we should spend our time and energies wisely. It is important that we cherish time with our families and friends, our neighbours and our colleagues, for the moments we share are precious and unrepeated. In recognising the time we have to share with others, we also acknowledge God's presence in those relationships too, and the precious gift of time we have been given.

Time to reflect

- on how we use our time
- on missed opportunities
- on quality time and memorable occasions
- on whether we are like Mary or Martha.

TIMING

3

Waiting patiently

Luke 2.25–32

Patience is a virtue, or so it is said. Perhaps it is said because it is something most of us lack, serving as a reminder to us of our impatience in daily life. We live very much in a culture where everything is on demand, and we expect to have our demands met, and in good time, thank you very much! It is a salutary thought, that despite all the time-saving devices that have been created over the years, we still seem to lack the time we need to do the things we want.

There is a wonderful image of patience to be found in the old western movies. People are found rocking in their chairs on porches, waiting for whatever will come round the corner. Rocking and waiting. Waiting and rocking.

When we think of Simeon, we might want to picture him as an old man rocking in his chair on the porch. He had been promised that he would see God's chosen one before he died, but time and life were moving on, and he just had to wait and wait. That is, until that day when Jesus was brought to the temple, and with delight Simeon was able to hold him in his arms, and say those memorable words: 'Now, Lord, let your servant depart in peace, for my eyes have seen your salvation.'

If only we could have the patience of Simeon, not just for all the big things in life, but also for the smaller things. God has blessed us in many ways, and has promised us his love and faithfulness for all time, but sometimes we are impatient with our lives, and the direction they seem to be taking.

Often in life, it is when we look back on what has gone before, that there is a greater sense of purpose to be found. Times of trial have brought something new to fruition. Times of wilderness have strengthened us for the journey. Times of loss have restored our faith in friendship and fellowship.

We, like Simeon, look to Christ for our salvation, and one day we will also see him and be held by him. For now, we have the gift of time, and the gift of life, to enjoy and to use wisely. May our waiting be a time of purpose, and our lives a testimony of faith like Simeon.

Time to reflect

- on what we are waiting for in life
- on how patient we are with God
- on times past that make greater sense now
- on the example of Simeon.

TIMING

4

Using time well

John 21.24-5

It's a fact of life that there are only 24 hours in a day, up to 31 days in a month, 12 months in a year, and once a year we gain an hour, and once a year we lose an hour, so nothing changes this equation. There are only so many hours in a day!

Of course, on a working day, many will wish that there weren't as many as 24 hours in a day, whereas on a day off, it's natural to wish for more time. There just doesn't seem to be enough time to allow us to do all that we want to do, or even need to do.

Isn't it reassuring then to know that it was the same for Jesus? He was acutely aware of the time he had to carry out his ministry, and he crammed it full of everything he could, so much so that there wasn't enough space to write down all he did. Presumably in the years after his ministry, as the Gospel of John was penned, it would have taken too long to write down everything because the important thing was to be spreading Jesus' message.

What John was able to do, however, was to give us a moving picture of the work of Jesus, and to give us a full account of his message, even if it had to be an edited one. John was clear in his writing to include the events that would lead the reader to understand that Jesus was the Son of God, and surely that was what was needed.

There is a message for all of us in our use of time – that it is important to include that which is most meaningful in our lives, and allow some of the other things to go. John didn't need to cram in every single detail of what Jesus did for us to understand who he was and how important his message was, as he was able to convey that in his twenty-one chapters adequately.

If we were to write a book about our lives, what would we include? No doubt it would be the significant and meaningful moments, the times where we learnt something about ourselves, or the world, and the journey that led us to the place we are now. We would probably leave out all the other insignificant details, and yet it is often these things that we spend our lives focused on.

To choose the better way, and to choose the best way to use our time is a daily challenge, but as we live our lives of faith, we are asked to make the time we have count, and not just to count for us, but to count for God too.

Time to reflect

- on how well we think we use our time
- on how we set our priorities
- on what priority our faith takes
- on what are the significant chapters in our own lives of faith.

UNITY

I

Being as one

Ephesians 4.1–6

One of the best things about going to the cinema, whether it is as a child or as an adult, is the opportunity to buy something to munch upon! Of course, popcorn is the main winner, but you only have to glance around to the 'pick and mix' selection of sweets to see the delight in 'children' of all ages as they pick and choose their favourites.

Society today is a bit of a pick and mix bag. We are encouraged at every turn to pick and choose, dependent on our preferences, whether that be choosing clothes, DVDs, electronic gadgets or what's for dinner. The choices are endless and where a consumer need is not met, it won't be long before a new product is born.

In this pick and mix life, what does it mean for us to hear the opening words of Ephesians 4? How do these words relate to our lives? 'There is one body, and one Spirit ... one hope ... one Lord, one faith, one baptism; one God and Father of all.' These words talk to us about unity – about unity in God, where all are one together through the bond of peace.

Such unity does not mean we are deprived of choice though, for the Christian faith is one of personal decision making and commitment, rather than a prescribed life. But in that life, there is the call of God, the challenge of God to be one. And what unites us? Why, faith, hope and God himself.

Amid all the other choices of this world and of our daily lives, God calls us to choose him and to live in him. To live in unity, not just for ourselves, but for the sake of all. We are asked to see that God offers the way for us, where there is a common bond shared by all who join the journey of faith.

So, returning to the cinema ... whether you would want to choose cola cubes and chocolate éclairs, or whether you would rather have fizzy cola bottles and bon bons, for the more serious pick and mix choices we have to make in life, God calls us to pick his way as the way for our lives, and not to mix it up with the many competing voices from the world around.

Time to reflect

- on daily choices that have to be made
- on poor choices we have made and lived with
- on times when we have ignored God's call
- on the challenge to live in unity.

UNITY

2

A common purpose

Acts 2.42–7

When you think about the Christian Church, do you think about
people living in harmony with each other? Do you think about
everybody sharing a common purpose and sharing everything
they have with one another? It is unlikely that you do, for sadly
the history of the Church is one of division and disagreement
which has been to the detriment of Christ's message.

The sort of community that is described at the beginning of
Acts is one that sounds idyllic, but also probably sounds unreal-
istic to most of us, and more akin to a new age eco-community
or something of the sort. But let us not be dismissive of this early
Christian community and their example, for there is something
attractive in their simplicity of sharing, and the sentiment of their
sincerity, and not least in their ability to attract others to join their
number. Perhaps, here is a glimpse of the ideal Christian community even if it was to be short lived.

Later in the New Testament we find in the letters of Paul to
various communities that things haven't quite continued in that
vein, and that arguments have arisen, and certain factions and
followings are causing some consternation. It is with some sadness that the original community has become like other Christian
communities and churches we know.

Yet, while there is sadness in recognising that, there is also the
confirmation of our human nature which is flawed and often at

fault, and therefore the reinforcement of our need of God, and of Christ's teaching in our lives. Ultimately of course, we find the need for our salvation repeated over and over again.

On one hand it is a hard thing to realise that we are all somewhat similar to the early Christians. We have our ideals and idealism, but in reality we often choose the way of division and disagreement. On the other hand, we are reminded powerfully again that unity is to be found in Christ alone, when we are connected to him, and allow his life to flow into ours.

We can only ever aspire to be Christ-like and to be like that early Christian community, but it is in the aspiration of that unity that we walk with Christ, and he walks with us.

Time to reflect

- on the failings of the Church
- on how we contribute to those failings
- on what we can learn from the early community
- on our need to rely on God's grace.

UNITY

3

Putting others first

Ruth 1.16–18

It is often a source of amusement that many football clubs use the word 'united' in their team name. One only has to watch the sports news each week to realise that in many ways that is a stretch of the imagination! Arguments between team members, fallouts with managers and trainers, not to mention occasional rifts on the pitch and fights with referees would seem to suggest that there isn't always the unity that one might want to see.

In true unity there is often self sacrifice. To be united means that one needs to put the need of the many before the individual need, and loyalty is a prize to be sought after. In terms of loyalty, this is where football supporters excel, as they usually follow their teams faithfully through the rough and the smooth.

When we look at the story of Ruth and Naomi, we find such an example of unity and loyalty and self sacrifice. Naomi's daughter in law, Ruth, pledges to go with her back to her homeland when widowed, even when she knows she will be treated as a foreigner and her prospects would be pretty grim. In those days, a woman's security was very much reliant on having a husband and Naomi knows that Ruth would be better going home to her own people, but cannot discourage her from coming with her.

In the modern world, full of jokes about mothers in law, this is an impressive example of love and devotion, and it is an example that goes on to find reward, for with Naomi's people, Ruth finds a new husband in Boaz, who has been moved by her faithfulness.

The principles at the heart of the story are principles for each of us as we try to live our lives in unity with one another. We need to work for unity within our personal lives, our working lives, and our lives of faith and service, and sometimes that unity will mean personal sacrifice and risk. However, the story reminds us not only that God goes with us through the rough and smooth of life, but that faithfulness is also rewarded.

The story of Ruth and Naomi stands the test of time as an example to all of us, in the choices we make in our lives. Ultimately it is an example of love, which puts others first.

Time to reflect

- on where our unity is tested
- on the need to make personal sacrifices at times
- on how Ruth must have felt making her choice
- on how we can learn from her example.

UNITY

4

Playing our part

1 Corinthians 12.12–13

When a child is born it is a wonderful moment in the life of a family. Babies are so perfectly formed, with their tiny fingernails and toes, that they are all beautiful, and made in the image and likeness of God. Watching a child grow is fascinating and amazing as they take in their first sights and sounds, as they begin to say their first words, and as they take their first steps. And of course, once they start walking and talking, there is little that will stop them!

It is little wonder that the symbol of the human body was used by Paul to convey how the Church should be. A body is indeed made up of many parts, and it is amazing to see how they function so well together to make us the people we are, living, breathing and acting in the world.

Of course bodies are not always perfect for many reasons, and indeed the Church, the body of Christ, is not always perfect either. There are times when one hand doesn't seem to know what the other is doing, there are times when the body seems to be working against itself, and there are times when it just seems to have lost its way.

The Church, though, is just made up of people like us, for we are the Church, the body of Christ, and we are the ones who often create disunity rather than harmony, and we are the ones who have the ability to make things better.

Paul's teaching about the body and unity is a profound piece of writing that transcends the passage of time and is immediately accessible for us all to understand. If one part of the body is suffering, so it all suffers, and so if one part rejoices, it all rejoices. It is a powerful picture of how the people of faith can be.

We should ask ourselves whether we really think of ourselves as being so integral to the whole body of Christ. Do we not often think that because we are only one, what we say and do will not really matter? Paul, and indeed God, would want us to realise that our part is of much greater significance than that.

It is only when people work together in faith and in common purpose that true unity is found. It is only when different people and different parts come together and find that what they share is more important than any division, that there can be true rejoicing. May we each play our part in bringing that to be.

Time to reflect

- on how we play our part in breaking unity
- on how we can play our part in bringing unity
- on which part of the body we most readily identify with
- on how it must pain God to see his Church divided.

PROVIDENCE

I

Plans and prosperity

Jeremiah 29.10–14

The television seems to be full of programmes about property – developing property, moving at home or abroad, selling houses, buying houses, transforming homes and decorating rooms. The thing they all seem to have in common is that they all require some measure of planning – whether it's planning permission from a council, or planning how colours might transform a room in reality. The other thing they all seem to have in common is that the plans never seem to run smoothly!

Perhaps that's not such a great surprise, because the patterns of life that we know are not always ones that run smoothly. No matter how much we plan and prepare, the unexpected can always happen, and what was once certain now becomes a new challenge or a frightening experience.

When Jeremiah spoke his words about God's plans and purpose in Chapter 29, he was speaking to those in exile to bring words of comfort and peace. 'For I know the plans I have for you, declares the Lord. Plans to prosper you and not to harm you, plans to give you hope and a future.' What wonderful words they must have been in the ears of the exiles – calming their fears and giving them new hope.

Of course there will be times in all our lives when we feel we are in exile of some sort. Where we feel disconnected from a life we formerly knew; where we feel unrooted and unable to relax;

where we are unsure of all that lies ahead. And into these times, Jeremiah's words come to me and to you, 'for I know the plans I have for you, says the Lord'.

Whether it is the stories of faith in the Old Testament, or whether it is in the lives of the first of Christ's disciples, there is a pattern that calls all who follow God to trust in his plans, even though we might not always understand where we are being led.

Each of us should hold onto the knowledge of God's presence and hear the voice of God echoing in our ears, bringing us out of our own times of personal exile, saying 'I have plans to prosper you and not to harm you, plans to give you hope and a future.'

Time to reflect

- on plans that have gone wrong
- on plans that remain unclear
- on where God might be calling us
- on Jeremiah's words for us today.

PROVIDENCE

2

God's guidance

Psalm 23

If you could choose to live your life over again as an animal, I wonder which animal you would choose. A common answer might be as a dog, for a well-looked-after dog enjoys everything with the wag of a tail, whether it is eating, sleeping or playing – or playing, eating and sleeping. It's not a bad life!

It's unlikely that many of us would choose to be a sheep as, apart from being warm and cosy in one's woollen coat, the assumption is that sheep are pretty stupid and just follow the crowd.

However, if you add into that picture the shepherd, the one who guards your life and looks after you with great care and attention, perhaps the life of a sheep is considered very blessed. In a way, the sheep is the obvious image of the Psalmist's time, just like a dog might be the chosen pet of our day.

Not surprisingly the loving image of the shepherd and his sheep became a powerful image of God's love for his people. It has helped people for centuries to understand the love of God in a rich and meaningful way, and has allowed people to see God's hand in their lives, guiding them through the dark valleys as well as the luscious and green pastures.

Often considered to be a Psalm appropriate to death, the Psalm is really more appropriate to life and the fullness of life at the heart of the Christian faith, for in Psalm 23 we find God at the heart of the whole of life, like a shepherd guiding his sheep.

Knowing that guidance of God in your life, and trusting in it, is a powerful thing. It has the power to give you confidence where life is shadowy and threatening, and gives the hope of better things to come. It has the power to promise you fulfilment in the daily path of life, but also the reminder of a future life in God where life finds its ultimate fulfilment.

The Psalm gives us an enduring image that has comforted and consoled in times past, and will do so for both the present and the future. We do not have to imagine living life in any other way, but are able to recognise the powerful image of God shepherding us, his sheep, in the pathways of life and faith.

Time to reflect

- on the image of the shepherd and his sheep
- on our relationship with God
- on the dark valleys of our lives
- on the places of rich pasture and promise.

PROVIDENCE

3

Relying on God

Matthew 7.7–12

How many of us, when we get lost trying to find somewhere, will stop and ask for directions? Most of us will rather try and rely on our own resources before admitting we need someone else's help! Of course in these days of satellite navigation systems there is less chance of getting lost, but perhaps there is even more chance of being led in the wrong direction! There are some amusing stories of such devices leading people to rivers where there are no bridges, or taking people on all sorts of weird and wonderful diversions.

Of course we can take ourselves on all sorts of diversions and routes in life, without considering the most obvious – to ask and to seek for advice. There is something within our own psyche that tends to want to rely on ourselves rather than anyone else.

Into that reality come the refreshing words of Christ. 'Ask and it will be given. Seek and you shall find. Knock and the door will be opened.' It sounds terribly inviting and easy, but is it really that simple?

As part of the Sermon on the Mount, Jesus encourages his followers to have a reliance on God, as they go about their lives. He continues to reinforce this teaching by giving examples of how we respond to the needs of our children, if we have them, and saying how much more God will give us, his children, the things we need when we ask him.

It takes a certain amount of faith to believe that God's providence will provide for us in such a perfect way, but Jesus encourages us to trust in God, in a new and deeper way, and not to rely on ourselves so much.

There is also a connection to be found here, in how we respond to the needs of others around us. When we recognise our need of God, and our own vulnerability, we are that much more open to the needs of others around us.

To do for others what you would have them do for you is a relationship of mutuality and respect and, importantly, Jesus says that this sums up the teaching of the Law and Prophets. Jesus is able to summarise for us all the teaching that has gone before into these basic principles.

Perhaps in the refreshing simplicity of his teaching we can consider again our reliance on God to show us his way, and therein find the pathway we should take in life.

Time to reflect

- on the times we have taken the wrong turn in life
- on where we need God's guidance
- on how we treat our neighbours
- on whether we are ready to ask, seek and knock.

PROVIDENCE

4

Being chosen

1 Peter 2.9–10

It's a great feeling when you are specially chosen to do something. From early days at school when a teacher singles you out in a positive way, to being chosen for a sports team, to being chosen after a job interview, to being chosen as a life partner, the times when we are chosen are truly meaningful to us.

In being chosen we are accorded a certain popularity and respect; we feel that we have been recognised and that we have been valued. In being chosen we have a greater sense of purpose in who we are, and what we can be, and we know that we have an important place in the grand scheme of things.

Consider then the enormous significance in knowing that we are chosen by God. God has chosen us to be a people belonging to him, a people that is chosen to bring praise and glory to his name, by living our lives for him.

What does it mean for us to be chosen by God? It means that God has welcomed us through his love and mercy and through his Son's saving work, to have a place in working out his kingdom. We have been chosen, but we also have a responsibility to respond to that invitation to be his people, for in God's providence we have always had the free will to choose.

Just as we feel valued in our everyday lives when we are chosen, so in our lives of faith, we find an inherent value in knowing that we have a place in God's plans, that we have a purpose as we walk the journey of life.

Often in life, we have the feeling that we are not making a difference, or that we do not know where things will lead or how things might work out. If we are able to hold within our hearts the belief that we have been chosen by God, and are loved in his everlasting love, we can be released to be the people God wants us to be more fully.

It is in knowing that we have a significant part to play in God's plan, that we have the confidence to live each day in faith and to God's glory.

Time to reflect

- on a time when we have been chosen
- on how it feels to be chosen by God
- on the plans we make in life
- on how we feel knowing we are part of God's plan.

CREATION

I

The beauty of the earth

Psalm 8

Take a moment to think about where your favourite place is ...
It might be a holiday destination, the top of a hill somewhere, a
favourite garden or beach, or a place that simply speaks to you ...

Most of us have a favourite place or many favourite places.
Somehow they are places that speak to us, whether in peaceful
tones, or by memories shared there, or through sheer unadult-
erated beauty. Many years ago, perhaps the Psalmist, the writer
of Psalm 8, stood in his favourite place and contemplated the
wonderful world that God had given.

And yet his wonder wasn't only about the inherent beauty
of the heavens – the moon and the stars in their place – but his
wonder was also that amid such splendour, God could consider
humanity and care for the people of the earth. Why in the midst
of a beautiful earth, would God choose ordinary folk to rule over
his creation?

How well we might ask that same question today, so many
years later, when the moon and stars are still held in their place,
but the earth is as tortured and troubled as it always was. What is
man that you care for him, O God?

When we consider together how human frailty and failing
continues to pollute the earth with greed and injustice, with fear
and oppression, with pain and prejudice, we might well question
God's good order in charging us with caring for his creation.

We are reminded again that it is not enough simply to enjoy the beauty of the earth, and encounter our favourite places, but that we have a responsibility to use the glory and honour with which we have been crowned to let the earth reveal God's majesty.

A beautiful tree was once transformed by the ugliness of nails when Christ was nailed to a cross, but then new life came forth. Amid the beauty of the world, let us not fail to see ugliness that needs to be transformed. Let us not shrink from the challenge of bringing forth new life, that the glory of God may be seen in heaven but also known on earth.

Time to reflect

- on the things we appreciate most in the world
- on the things we close our eyes to
- on the places where we can make a difference
- on our commitment to go and do so.

CREATION

2

On eagles' wings

Isaiah 40.28–31

No-one likes to be left out of knowing things that other people know. We don't like to feel that we are missing out on something, and don't have access to the same information as others. When we are holding information then there's nothing better than being able to share it with others, is there? Some might even call it gossiping!

Well the prophet Isaiah didn't want to leave anything to chance when it came to conveying God's message to people. 'Do you not know? Have you not heard?' he asked. 'Because if you don't know and if you haven't heard, then listen now, and I will tell you.' What Isaiah had to tell, though, was not gossip. It was far more important than that. It was a message about God's nature and God's nurture.

In a passage that begins with God's comfort to his people, Isaiah goes on to emphasise the eternal nature of God, the one who has created all things.

It is a wonderful thing to think about this eternal God, who never tires or wearies as we do. Imagine how good it must be to have that everlasting energy that can turn the negative to the positive, and can restore that which is needing to be refreshed.

Who of us would not like to recover the energy of our youth, to see things again with fresh eyes, as if for the first time? Perhaps then we might accept things in a different and fuller way. The words of Isaiah call us to hear about God and his creation again in a fresh and new way.

Here, we find renewal of our energies, like soaring eagles. Here, we find fresh promise of hope and encouragement to go forth in the power of God, who has made us his creation, and strengthens us by his Spirit.

We have good news to share and we, like Isaiah, must be willing to share the information we have about our wonderful Creator God. Do you not know? Have you not heard? Then let me be sure to tell you, that 'The Lord is the everlasting God, the Creator of the ends of the earth.'

Time to reflect

- on the beauty of God's creation
- on the places where our energy is renewed
- on the message we have to share
- on the everlasting power of God with us.

CREATION

3

A *new creation*

2 Corinthians 5.17–20

There is something quite exciting about getting something new. It might be a new car, a new sofa, or just some new clothes, but it is the newness that makes it special. You might have loved the item that was being replaced, but still, something new has a certain look and feel to it, that can't be replicated by something old. No wonder shopping seems to be a national pastime!

Do you ever think of yourself as new, though? More than likely, you think of yourself in the opposite way! We are all conscious of how the years seem to pass quicker as we age, and how we don't have the same energy and youthful enthusiasm we might have had in days gone by. We are glad to know that every morning is new with God, but we are not so sure about feeling new ourselves!

Yet we find these words of challenge in Paul's letter to the Corinthians; that we are a new creation in Christ. In Christ the old has gone and the new has come. Do we really feel that within ourselves? Do we really feel changed and transformed deep down? Do we consider that we have been given life anew?

The phrase 'to be born again' is one that is open to abuse, but it is a strong image to think of the Christian life as one that brings a new birth and a new way of being into our lives. Paul describes it in a healing way, rather than a demanding way, by saying that we have been reconciled with God through Christ's death, so that a new relationship with God can begin.

When we are able to root this teaching into a relationship, perhaps the call to be a new creation can be helpfully explained. In any new relationship, whether it be one of love or friendship, or even in a working relationship with colleagues, there is initial excitement and energy to build on the new, and to develop a meaningful and lasting relationship.

Perhaps at its most simple, we are called by God to have that same attitude to being a new creation in him. We are invited to have that new excitement and energy and dedication as we build on our relationship with God, never forgetting how it has been gifted to us.

Just as we love getting something new, we are reminded that there is nothing we should love more than this new opportunity to grow in relationship with God, and to be a new creation.

Time to reflect

- on what is old and tired in our lives
- on something new that has brought us excitement
- on whether we have the same excitement about our relationship with God
- on our need to find that newness in our life of faith.

CREATION

4

God in and around us

Psalm 121

It is hard not to be moved by the beauty of creation at times. While the earth has its barren places, there are so many places of extreme beauty, discovered and undiscovered, which give us cause to stop and to stare and to consider our part within the whole of creation.

The Psalmist was very much in touch with the created world, for his life was much more tied to the seasons and the earth than our modern-day lives of comparative comfort. It was in the sun's rising and setting and the knowledge of God's presence with him each day, that he was able to praise God for the wonder and help that surrounded him.

In the Celtic tradition of spirituality there was also this close tie between creation and blessing in the fragile existence of life. Prayers were spoken for all sorts of things, from the lighting of lamps to the milking of cows, in the understanding that God was simply part of everything in life. It is an understanding we can learn from as we go about our daily life, often oblivious to the God that walks with us.

When the Psalmist looked to the hills, he thought of God's help surrounding him and strengthening him. He saw in the beauty of creation a picture of the beauty of God, who had created him and given him his life.

Sometimes we close our minds off to what the world around us can teach us. In the setting and rising of the sun, we can know the blessing of a new day and the promise of God with us. In the wonder of creation, we can learn about the wonder of God who has provided so much richness and beauty. In the coolness of a breeze we can call to mind the Spirit of God, moving in and through us, and in the changing of the seasons, we can reflect on the changing patterns of our own lives.

The Psalmist reminds his readers that while we sleep at night, God never rests and is always with us. It is a remarkable image that has brought comfort over the centuries to many who have gone before us in faith.

Let us then open our hearts and minds again to the world around us, for creation reveals something to us of God, and his relationship with us, for we are part of his creation.

Time to reflect

- on the beauty of the world we know
- on the blessing of each new day
- on the presence of God in creation
- on the promise of God always to be with us.

GROWTH

I

New shoots

John 15.1–8

Living in a colder climate, we are not so used to seeing vines and branches bearing great bundles of fruit. Perhaps we are more used to the produce of these vines in bottles we enjoy – red, white, sparkling and rosé! Yes, surely it is a good thing that a vine bears fruit!

Perhaps if Jesus had lived in our green and pleasant land, with archetypal old houses amid rolling fields and country lanes, he might have drawn his attention to the imagery of ivy instead.

Ivy can be such a beautiful plant, growing colourfully and quickly, covering walls and roofs and hanging down over windows to picturesque effect. But it can also be a persistent plant, for its tendrils make their way into every little nook and cranny, holding on firmly, that the ivy might grow and grow, and be quite difficult to remove in time.

However, that may be a good image for the Christian life when it comes to growth. The opportunity to beautify that which is around with the good news and love of God, but also the persistent ability to spread into the little-known places, the dark places, the hidden places and put down roots of faith where they can't necessarily be seen.

True faith should keep growing and keep spreading, seen and unseen, and it should be difficult to hold it back, to cut it back, to hamper its growth. Jesus spoke of being the vine and his followers being the branches, that connected together there would be growth and there would be fruit to be seen and enjoyed by others.

So are we firmly rooted in Christ? Are we drawing our nourishment from him, that we are able to grow and spread his word? Are we like a vine that bears good fruit? Are we like the ivy, creeping into all the dark spaces that need Christ's light?

Whatever we are, we should be growing – fed and nourished by God's word, and reaching out to bring blessing to others. 'Remain in me, and I will remain in you. No branch can bear fruit by itself.'

Time to reflect

- on whether we continue to grow in God
- on times when we have stood still
- on when we forget we are rooted in God
- on the desire to bear fruit for God.

GROWTH

2

Making a difference

Matthew 28.16–20

When children are learning about how things grow in school, they are often encouraged to sow some cress or mustard seeds, or even a sunflower seed, so that they might monitor its growth and see the results. There wouldn't be much point in choosing a very slow-growing plant as there wouldn't be much to see after a while, and it would hardly keep a child's interest.

As adults, we are not much different. We like to see results and see something fruitfully growing from our labours, whether that be in doing the garden, or working on some project, or learning something new. We are encouraged when we see growth and improvement, and it spurs us on to do more.

It's little wonder then that sometimes our communities of faith grow a bit tired and despondent when growth is difficult to measure, and yet the great commission of Jesus remains the same; to go out and make disciples of all nations.

Throughout much of the world the Christian Church continues to grow, yet in the west there is a rather different picture. It would be wrong to say that there is no growth, for there are many faithful shoots flourishing, but the institutional Church as we know it continues to suffer decline and a reduced and ageing membership.

Perhaps the clue is in the word 'institutional', for once anything becomes part of an institution there is greater inflexibility and more rules and regulations. As such, it is refreshing to hear again the simplicity of Jesus' call to go out and make disciples of all nations, baptising them, and teaching them Christ's way.

It is difficult to measure growth in any other way than numbers, but it is clear that there is a growth in spirituality in the western world if not in Christianity, and there is an opportunity for the Church as we know it to break out of its present mould and meet people with Christ's commission in a down-to-earth and meaningful way. After all, Christ walked where people were going about their everyday lives, and talked to people in everyday ways they would understand.

We have much to learn from the simplicity of Christ's ministry and, in faith, we will never fully know how the seeds we sow may grow. Ultimately, we are called to faithfully share the gospel, and being faithful to that calling is more important than measuring results, and God believes each one of us is able to make a difference, even if we don't have the same faith in ourselves!

Time to reflect

- on the barriers to growth we see in our own lives
- on the barriers we see to growth in our Church
- on how we can make small and simple differences
- on what we can learn from new shoots of growth.

GROWTH

3

Continuing the work

Matthew 9.35–8

When you want a job done, then ask a busy person! It's often true that the busy people are the ones to achieve things quicker than those who walk through life at a calmer pace. All of us feel the pressures of getting things done on time, and getting things done properly, and it is often in delegating responsibility to someone else that some of the pressures can be relieved, and the task gets done.

Jesus must have felt quite overwhelmed at times with the crowds that flocked to hear him and to be close to him. He was only one man, albeit the Son of God, but one person just the same. The years of his ministry were short, only three, and in that time he went many places and touched many people's lives, but the crowds kept coming, even when he was trying to find some space to be at prayer by himself.

Despite coming under such pressure, Jesus never lost his compassion for those who came to him. He engaged with people wherever he went, responding to their needs, bringing healing and teaching about God's kingdom, but he recognised that he could not do it all.

Jesus knew his limitations, and yet he knew the need was great. He must have been conscious of how short his time was, knowing all that lay ahead, and he was keen to teach his disciples that they had the power and authority to go out in his name and do his work.

That is an important message for us as current-day disciples of Christ, for his work of declaring God's kingdom and living out its values must continue in our lives. We are called to be his hands and feet, serving in the world.

Jesus reminds his followers that there is much opportunity out there for spreading the good news, and allowing God's kingdom to grow. 'The harvest is plentiful, but the workers are few,' he says.

Is that not a call to each of us, to continue in faith, striving to be Christ-like, and allowing his kingdom to grow? There are many who need to hear his message, and who need to find wholeness therein and, although we are often busy people, Jesus wants his work to continue. He has delegated to us this task, and we must rise to the challenge.

Time to reflect

- on how we use our time
- on how we can continue Christ's work
- on where the harvest is plentiful
- on what God is calling us to do.

GROWTH

4

From small beginnings

Mark 4.30–2

Good things come in small packages! Well, some of us would like to think so anyway! Anyone who is a little short in stature holds onto that theory with great hope, and there is certainly some truth in it.

The mustard seed is one of the smallest seeds around, and if you buy a packet of them in a garden centre you will find that the contents are in excess of 1,000 normally, providing lots of seeds for very little money.

The type of mustard seed Jesus was talking about in his parable about the kingdom of God wasn't dissimilar to those we would buy today. From a very small seed could grow a large plant that was able to give welcome shade to the birds round about it. Using the geography and environment round about him, Jesus was able to explain to those who were listening to his teaching, how God's kingdom could grow from something small using an example they would readily understand.

Many of us are quite disparaging about the smallest coins of our British currency. The 1p and the 2p are often used for nothing other than storing up in jam jars or charity boxes until they add up to something of greater value. But you only need 100 pence to make up a pound, and you only need a few pounds to make a difference in the world. If you look at the developing world, a few pounds can be used, for example, to buy chickens which can turn a family's fortunes around by not only providing food, but a means of farming and trading. So perhaps if we watch the pennies, the pounds can really look after themselves!

Jesus' parable about the mustard seed reminds us that in God's kingdom, even the smallest thing can grow into something meaningful, whether that be a seed of faith, a seed of love, or a seed of hope. In God's kingdom, growth can come from the most insignificant offering.

We often place higher value on the bigger things in life, but Jesus' parable reminds us to trust that with God, the smallest thing can have a powerful effect. It is often in the little things that we say and do, that God's kingdom comes nearer.

Time to reflect

- on how the seeds of faith have grown in our lives
- on small changes that have been of significance
- on how God calls us to see potential in all
- on our place in making God's kingdom grow.

SERVICE

I

Crossing boundaries

John 13.1–17

There are boundaries that we all have in our minds to what we think is right and proper. We don't expect an old person to give up a seat for a young person on a bus; we don't expect a surgeon to bring us our breakfast when we are in hospital; we don't expect a waitress to wash our hands before we eat.

Jesus' disciples had their own ideas and boundaries too, and the only person who should have been washing feet was a servant or slave. It was a pretty grotty job with all the dirt and dust that was around, and there were rules about these things, or so they thought!

Yet, in a moving account, we read how Jesus challenged his disciples' thinking by washing their feet. Taking on the role of a servant, he knelt before them and washed them each in turn. But not only that, in doing so, he set them an example to follow – an example that would call them to go forward in faith and break down society's rules and boundaries in Christ's name.

What does it mean to serve in such a revolutionary way? What does it mean to do something similar today? We are each being called to do the unexpected; to do that which another would not do; to do that which does not always make sense in the world's eyes, and to display in our lives the truth that in God's sight we are all equal.

As Christians, our lives should display the love of Christ, and if his example was to kneel and wash the feet of his disciples, then we must be reminded that our faith should shake us from a complacent life to a life of service – of giving not in order to receive – of serving, because it is what Christ would do. We are called to surprise others with the love of God, in a world where folk are suspicious of anything that is freely given.

Time to reflect

- on opportunities for service
- on the times we have failed to serve
- on the example of Jesus for our lives
- on the challenge to live by faith.

SERVICE

2

Role reversal

Mark 9.33–7

Picture the scene: you are in the local supermarket and there is a queue at every checkout and people are getting a little agitated as they wait to be served. An announcement comes over the PA system apologising for the delay and asking people to be understanding. That seems to help. But a moment later a further announcement is made, asking people to reverse their position in the queue, so that those at the front return to the end of the queue. It doesn't take much imagination to know that chaos and consternation would follow!

We all like to have our place in life, whether it is our rightful place in the supermarket queue or whether it is our status within our working life. So too, in our family life, we are accorded some internal rank of seniority, and in groups we are part of, we also like to know where we stand.

Human nature being what it is, it is hardly surprising to find two of Jesus' disciples arguing about who was the greatest. It is not surprising, even if it is disappointing, and truly, Jesus must have felt some disappointment in them too.

As Jesus' first disciples, perhaps the group felt that they should have some special status and standing. How surprised and deflated they must have felt when Jesus tried to explain that the first would be the last, and would be a servant of all. The status of a servant in Jesus' time was nothing to be desired at all.

Jesus then continues to add insult to injury by giving a high status to children, who were, I am sure, just as noisy and unpredictable in his day as they are in ours. Surely Jesus was being mis-guided!

It is a powerful transformation of priorities that Jesus gives in this teaching about who is the greatest. It turns our ideas on their head, and challenges us to see the reversal of the queue in the supermarket as being indicative of how Christ expects us to serve others, by putting them first and not counting the cost.

Yes, it challenges our sensibilities, and radically gives a picture of a kingdom which is at odds with the world that we know. Surely that is the point though. Perhaps if we were living as the oppressed and the poor, such teaching would inspire our living with hope. However, for those of us who are blessed with status in the world as it is, in terms of wealth and freedom, Christ's words remain as challenging today as they did when first uttered. We must look again to his example, and learn how to serve as he has served.

Time to reflect

- on how we would have felt hearing these words of Jesus' for the first time
- on how Jesus' words challenge our daily living
- on how we can begin to respond to the challenge
- on how we might be able to serve others.

SERVICE

3

Living by example

James 2.14–19

Imagine attending a conference where a leading international peace activist is addressing the assembled crowd on the need for establishing peaceful communities in the world, where mutual respect and understanding flourishes. He delivers a powerful address, stirring his hearers into positive action, instilling in them the belief that peaceful living begins with individuals, filters into communities, and such positivity can be multiplied in the world.

After leaving the stage, the speaker is rude to the backstage assistant who forgot to provide his bottle of sparkling water on stage, he pushes past another backstage person who is in his way, and then goes on to berate his manager publicly for not making sure things were set up to his satisfaction. It doesn't add up does it? What use is it to be saying one thing and then doing the other?

The Salvation Army holds a great deal of respect in the minds of many people, Christian or otherwise, for throughout the years, despite their motto of 'blood and fire', their enduring image is one of practical action. The work of the Salvation Army is often seen in the running of soup kitchens, or housing the homeless, or running shelters for addicts among other things. They show their Christian love in practical action.

The letter of James is full of common-sense teaching for those who would live the Christian life. He calls people to account for their faith by their actions, and says that without actions, faith is dead. Strong words indeed.

There are many examples of Christian love in action that have powerfully influenced others; Mother Theresa of Calcutta is an obvious example. Through her work, and her ability to show others that her work was carried out because of her faith, she has been, and continues to be, an inspiration to others.

We, who are Christians, may never be able to rise to the same high example of faith as Mother Theresa but, in everyday words and actions, we have the opportunity and the choice to show our faith by the way we live our lives.

Christ calls us to serve other people by getting involved in doing, rather than just saying. After all, he set a great example in his own life, by supporting his teaching in the way he lived and acted. May the words of James encourage us to do the same.

Time to reflect

- on times when our words and actions don't match
- on the need for forgiveness
- on the challenge to make our faith active
- on good examples for us to follow.

SERVICE

4

Christ who serves

Luke 22.14–20

Many significant occasions in our lives have been shared around food: birthday parties, anniversaries, Christmas dinners, New Year celebrations, funeral teas. The list could be endless. Whenever people gather together socially, there is usually food to bind them together.

The significance of sharing food together has been picked up by church discipleship groups, who invite those who are exploring the Christian message to gather for a meal and fellowship prior to any discussion. There is good method in this, as relaxing over food can allow one to gel with a group, and can help a deeper engagement and level of comfort in exploring the faith together.

Of course, the most famous meal shared in the Christian story is that of Jesus' last supper with his disciples. This was a highly emotionally charged meal. Not only was it the annual Passover festival, it was at a time when Jesus was coming close to the end of his earthly life, knowing that Judas was soon to betray him, but keen to explain to his disciples the love he had for them.

He took the everyday symbols of bread and wine to explain to his disciples what he was about to do in the giving of his life, in the breaking of his body, and the shedding of his blood. He helped them to understand why he must die and how all who would follow after him should remember him through these symbols of bread and wine.

It is the highest form of service to give one's life for another, and in the giving of his life Jesus was serving all who would want to restore their relationship with God. By dying to share the truth about God's love, not willing or able to compromise his message, Jesus brought salvation to all who would believe in his name.

We are used to being served by others when we go out for a meal with family or friends, but in this meal shared with his disciples, Jesus served us, and continues to serve us by his very life. It is when we share bread and wine together in his name that we recall his sacrifice, and we are nourished and fed so that we might go forward in faith, to serve as Christ has served us.

Time to reflect

- on the symbols of bread and wine
- on the emotions present at the last supper
- on the salvation offered in Christ
- on the call to serve others.

JUSTICE

I

Standing up and speaking out

Luke 4.14–21

Whenever we want to state our case strongly about something, we might be described as being on our soapbox. The term refers to the use of a box to stand on in places like Speakers' Corner, where if someone had something they wanted others to hear, they would stand tall and make their voice heard. What drives you to your soapbox? Is it taxes? The cost of petrol? The state of society? Poverty and injustice?

One day in Nazareth, where Jesus had grown up as a boy, he went to the synagogue, and there he got on his soapbox – or more accurately, he read from the scroll of Isaiah. And reading from that scroll, about freeing the oppressed and bringing good news to the poor, Jesus set out his stall, so to speak – he said, 'This is what I am about.'

Jesus never seemed to have any qualms about stating his case, but then he was God's chosen one. It must have taken courage and some audacity to stand before others in the synagogue and tell them that what the prophet Isaiah had said would come true through him. That's how to anger the religious authorities pretty quickly!

But how often do we have the same courage of our convictions? How often in our Christian lives do we stand up for what we know to be right and to be true? Are we more likely to keep our mouths shut, afraid of upsetting the apple cart and causing friction?

Jesus called his followers to live in the world, but not be of the world and, by telling all who would follow after him that his focus was on the poor and the oppressed, he was setting out a radical path to follow. His life would be marked out by justice and service, but inevitably this would lead to unpopularity and persecution.

There was nothing that could deter Jesus from his path, faithfully following God's plans and purposes for him, even if it led to a cross. Nothing would compromise his ultimate trust in the goodness of God and the message of God's love.

But what about you and me? Are we able to grasp hold of this radical calling to share in Christ's way of justice? We are asked to stand tall, to face our fears, to nail our colours to the post, and declare by our faith and works whose we are and whom we serve.

Time to reflect

- on what issues of justice we are passionate about
- on the times when we hide our convictions
- on the challenge to stand firm in faith
- on the invitation to share in Christ's work.

JUSTICE

2

Being accountable

Amos 5.11–12, 22–4

Most of us like to consider ourselves as good people. There is nothing wrong in that. Hopefully many of us are indeed good people in the sight of others, and long may it continue to be so. The world needs good people.

Remembering the teaching that 'man looks at the outward appearance, while God looks at the heart', it is perhaps a more difficult question to ask whether God would consider us as good people. There is no intention here to offend, but what is it that makes someone good?

Is it being kind and considerate? Is it attending church? Is it about being the best you can be? Is it about putting other people first? Surely one could argue it could be any or all of these things. However, what if you are kind and considerate, a regular worshipper at church, and conscious of serving others, and yet you are violent towards your spouse? Or maybe you have investments that benefit your finances but which fund arms in the developing world? Or maybe you think that homeless folk and asylum seekers are a blight on society? For all your goodness, what would God see?

From the words of Amos, we find a wake-up call to all who would praise God with worship and sacrifice, but who would trample on the poor and deprive people of justice. For here we find that God abhors such hypocrisy and calls people to account for their lives and their actions, and not just people in general, as his words are addressed to God's chosen people, Israel.

As Christians, we are a chosen people, for we are called children of God, and that requires an acknowledgement on our behalf that our lives must be accountable to God, as well as to our fellow human beings. Of course we should be seen to be good people, but that goodness must also be seen by God. It is not enough to say one thing and do the other. Our God requires more of us.

Those who consider Christianity an easy path, or a prop for life, are sorely mistaken, for we are each challenged to live our lives justly and rightly in the sight of God, and that is no easy path.

Time to reflect

- on whether we are good people
- on what areas of our life need to change
- on the blessing of knowing God's presence
- on how we might respond to God's call for justice.

JUSTICE

3

The gift of forgiveness

Matthew 18.21–35

It is the easiest thing to hold a grudge. Despite something hurtful happening a long time ago, despite our apparent forgiveness of the one who caused the upset, it is very difficult for us not to store up some resentment and bring it out as ammunition on occasion. We have all seen it happen among family or friends, when something from the past comes to rear its ugly head, and strains relationships and brings tension.

The parable of the Unforgiving Servant is a stark example of such things, and helps to put Jesus' teaching in a context we can understand. The indignity we feel as we hear about this horrible man who is forgiven and will not forgive, seems at first an obvious tale of a bad character who deserves whatever he gets. There is an obvious example of justice at issue.

However, the parable is about forgiveness, and an illustration of how often we might forgive someone. Peter's question, of how often he might be required to forgive his brother before he had passed the point of no return, seems quite a straightforward question to begin with. In answering it, though, Jesus confronts each of us with our own lives, and how often we might need to be forgiven.

While the unforgiving servant might not be a character we can readily recognise within ourselves, we can see in his story how the parable relates to the forgiveness that each of us needs from God for the many times we fall short in our lives. How often should God forgive us? Indefinitely, we pray and hope! And yet, if we are to be forgiven so freely, how much more then are we to forgive those who sin against us?

The nature of forgiveness is a complicated matter, for it has so many strands and has such wide-ranging effect on the lives of individuals and communities. Whether it be a family feud, a terrorist bombing, a matter of unfaithfulness or a wrongful imprisonment, there are many complicated issues at stake. Justice is served when accountability is its partner, and this is borne out in the parable we have.

God has freely offered his love, and through our faith in Christ we find forgiveness. We have been treated more than justly by God, and are required to live our lives in that knowledge, letting it affect how we might respond to those issues of justice and forgiveness that arise in our own individual lives.

Time to reflect

- on grudges that we continue to hold
- on whether we can find it in our hearts to forgive
- on the forgiveness God has granted to us
- on how justice should guide our living.

JUSTICE

4

Transforming injustice

Luke 19.1–10

You have to admire people for their effort when they go to great lengths to get something. Each year people queue outside Wimbledon for tickets to see the tennis, some even spending a night or two under canvas to get the tickets they want. Whenever a new computer games console comes out, you will also see people queuing for hours to be one of the first to get hold of it. The same is true when it comes to getting concert tickets for a big event, or when an eagerly awaited book or film comes out. Many of us would not dream of going to such extreme lengths, but you have to take your hat off to those who do!

If we had been Zacchaeus, and we wanted to see Jesus but found we couldn't because of the gathered crowd, would we have thought to climb the tree like he did, or would we have thought it was a waste of time and turned and gone home? Perhaps it's hard to know what we might have done.

However, Zacchaeus' effort is duly rewarded when Jesus notices him and invites himself to his house. There is a sense of justice in Jesus taking the time not only to notice, but to spend time with this tax collector: after all, he had made a special effort.

Of course the crowd didn't see it that way, and they were incensed that Jesus would choose to go and dine with this sinner, for tax collectors were well known for their abuse of power in creating their own wealth.

There is a further sense of justice in how the meeting with Jesus encourages Zacchaeus to consider his faults. He has been so moved by Jesus affording him his attention and welcome that he considers the error of his ways, and promises to rectify the situation.

Justice is served that day, for not only do Zacchaeus and the rest of the crowd discover that God's love extends to all, including the sinner, but that it also requires a just response.

Zacchaeus is to be admired for his effort and his openness to seeing the error of his ways, and his story is a challenge to each of us that we might do the same.

Time to reflect

- on the times when we sin
- on where we allow injustice to prevail
- on the love of God for us
- on our willingness to change.

LOVE

I

The gift of forgiveness

John 21.15-19

There is a statue of Jesus and Peter by the side of Lake Galilee at a place called Mensa Christi. Here, Jesus appeared to his disciples following the resurrection, and here, Jesus reinstated Peter following his denial. Early in the morning, when the sun is low in the sky and the light is shimmering on the lake the sculpture of Jesus and Peter is as powerful an image of love as one can imagine.

If you can think of a time in your life when you have let someone down badly, then perhaps you have been fortunate enough to have known their forgiveness. If you can think of a time when you have failed someone, then perhaps you still live with that pain and unresolved disappointment. It is human nature to fall below the standards we would want for ourselves, and our God would want for us.

It is hard to imagine the disappointment that Peter must have felt when Jesus predicted he would deny him three times. It is even harder to imagine the pain that Peter must have felt when, three times, from his own mouth, he said 'I do not know him', and then in the distance heard a cock crowing.

To fail another human being is a grave thing indeed, but to fail one's Lord at a time of great trial must have been almost too hard to bear. Only the greatest love could rescue Peter from his torment.

And there, by Galilee, where the greatest love overcame death to bring new life, we find Jesus reinstating Peter. He asks him three times, 'Do you love me?', each time cleansing him of the pain of his denial. Three times he asks, and three times Peter answers. It is the act of greatest love that not only forgives, but says to Peter, 'Feed my sheep.'

It is the act of greatest love that Christ our Lord forgives both you and me for all our sins, but not only that: he brings us into a new relationship with him, where there is a plan and purpose for our lives. If it is not enough that Christ forgives us in love, he then goes on to give us a task to do. His love is so great that it both calls us and sends us – it reinstates us to a place where we are held and known and loved by God.

From Peter's reinstatement, he went on to be the rock on which the Church was built. From our forgiveness we are called to be the body of Christ, loving and serving in the world.

Time to reflect

- on where we need God's forgiveness
- on where we know we have failed
- on the wonder of God's love and mercy
- on the opportunity to feed Christ's sheep.

LOVE

2

The gift of extravagance

John 12.1–8

Sometimes it is good to be extravagant! There are occasions in life where it is better not to count the cost of something because the gift will be so meaningful or memorable. Such occasions of extravagance can be anything from sending flowers to someone who will be over the moon to receive them, to paying for a holiday that might be someone's last, to giving a gift just because you love someone, rather than because they deserve something.

It is often said that you can't go wrong by buying women perfume, but you don't often hear of women giving perfume away! But in this story of extravagance, Mary is found anointing Jesus with an expensive perfume much to Judas' annoyance. It is hard to imagine a bottle of perfume costing the equivalent of a year's wages, but here we find just such a sacrifice being made in devotion to Jesus.

It's likely that many of us would have had the same reaction as Judas, though. We might even imagine that Jesus would agree that it was better to use the money for the poor as well. But what Mary was doing for her Lord was so extravagant in love, and so symbolic in meaning, that it was not a time to count the cost.

It is a moving image, to think of Mary anointing Jesus' feet with the perfume and wiping them with her hair. It is even more memorable when one realises that this was symbolic of the anointing of Jesus prior to his death to come. By doing such a thing,

Mary was giving her devotion to Jesus without counting the cost. It was an act of the moment, and one that meant a great deal to Jesus, and it was an offering that filled the whole house that night with the fragrance of her devotion.

How might we have shown our love for Jesus in this time leading up to the cross? Might we have been cynical like Judas? Might we have been all bravado and then cowardly like Peter, or might we have been extravagant like Mary?

We should always be extravagant in our love for God, by loving with heart, mind, soul and strength, and in loving our neighbour too. How we live our lives should be as permeating as that fragrance that Mary poured out. How we love should be a flowing of God's love through us, affecting and infecting all we say and do.

There are times to be frugal and cautious, but there are times to be extravagant in love, just as Christ spent his whole life and being for us on the cross.

Time to reflect

- on times when we are extravagant
- on how we might be extravagant for God
- on the love showed for us on the cross
- on the example Mary set us.

LOVE

3

Accepting difference

Matthew 5.43–8

It is a wonderful thing that we are all created differently. Even identical twins will have their own personality, and life would be quite boring if we were all the same. From our early years of nurture as children we begin to grow into our skin, so to speak, and we develop who we are and grow our own distinct personality.

On the negative side, as we differ from other people, so too, from early years, we often mark out people who don't belong in our environment. We choose who to be friends with, we choose who to ignore and, sadly, we also choose those to dislike.

It is hard for us to go against the grain and choose to befriend those who do not quite fit our mould, whatever that might be, and it is even harder to love those whom we struggle to like. Taking this even further, we find Jesus telling us to love our enemies and to pray for those who persecute us.

Hopefully, in most of our lives, we might not consider that we have enemies, but for those who serve in the Armed Forces in places of war and conflict, enemies are a definite reality. If we consider how difficult it is to love those we dislike, then this has to be multiplied many times to understand what it is to love your enemy.

In his words, Jesus was trying to teach his followers to depart from the traditional teaching of hating one's enemies. He was trying to establish a new order which understands that God's love is for all, and that Christian love requires going the extra mile. There is nothing distinctive about Christ's followers if they only do that which others do. Christ tells us that more is required.

We might not have true enemies in life, but we frequently exclude others, or look down our noses at people, dismissing them with ease. Even the Church is not exempt from such bad practice.

Just as Christ's love stretches out to the very least, so our lives are to show and share his love, despite our natural reservations. We are to take hold of this new teaching and apply it to living as Christ lived.

Time to reflect

- on who are our enemies
- on why we hold such views
- on the challenge to love
- on the ways we need to change.

LOVE

4

The greatest commandment

Mark 12.28–31

It seems that there is nothing in life that now happens without some sort of law to govern it. We now live in a truly litigious society which requires us to be warned that the contents of a coffee cup will be hot, and that requires a risk assessment to be done for even the most nominal of tasks. Walk into a law library and you will be overwhelmed by the number of statutes that govern our life and our living. Look further, and you will also be amazed at how the language of legal documents is enough to terrify even the well educated.

It wasn't terribly different in Jesus' time when there were so many religious laws to follow that people struggled to remember them all, and different religious groups gave greater weight to some than others. The same could be said of religious groups today who might pick and choose laws, particularly from the books of the Old Testament, to legitimise their support for a cause or their prejudice against it.

We should all be eternally grateful to the teacher of the law who asked Jesus which was the most important commandment of them all. Jesus didn't even seem to hesitate to answer, that loving God with your whole being was the first commandment, and loving your neighbour as yourself was the second. It is good to repeat again that he said, 'No other commandment is greater than these.'

Jesus, as ever, was able to cut through all the complications to utter in everyday words what was most important at the heart of faith in God. It was simply this: it was love.

It is such an obvious and common-sense double bill of commands, which sadly often gets confused in the living of the Christian life. There is far too much weight given to differences of interpretation and opinion between Christian denominations. What are we, if we have not love?

If we were to ask Jesus the same question today as that teacher of the law, among all the competing voices of the world, Jesus would repeat his answer with clarity, reminding us that there is no greater command than these.

If we were able to live our lives truly in that belief and knowledge, then surely Christ's disciples would be known by their love.

Time to reflect

- on the simplicity of Christ's answer
- on where we are less than loving
- on the need to hear Christ's answer again
- on how we can live out God's love.

LIFE

I

Signs of faith

Mark 1.14–20

Have you ever been quietly going about your own business and all of a sudden, something comes and shatters everything you have known? Perhaps you have heard wonderful news, and it changes how you might view the future. Perhaps you have heard devastating news and are unsure of how to respond. The events of life are often unchartered, and it is a blessed life that is not shaken at some point in time.

It is hard to imagine how Simon and Andrew felt that morning that Jesus turned their lives upside down. It had just been an ordinary day, and they were just going about their usual task, and he walked by. Well, he didn't just walk by – he challenged them to follow him, and offered a life of catching people. How intriguing!

Unless Simon and Andrew were less than human, the Gospel account misses out something. Surely, they can't have followed after Jesus without some moment of indecision – some strange sideways glances at each other to check if this man really meant it. Perhaps there was a shrug of the shoulders to say, 'What have we to lose?', before they took up the invitation that would change their lives for ever.

Do we sometimes feel that our lives of faith have lacked that momentous decision? For many of us, faith has been a gradual journey from childhood, and even for those for whom there has been a great moment of decision, it is unlikely that it led to such a radical change as for Simon and Andrew. After all, how many of us have left behind our livelihoods, our homes and our families for our faith?

But what this calling of the first disciples teaches us is that Christ's call comes to us amid the daily things of this life – among the everyday work that we do. And it is perhaps here that we can serve Christ to our best ability, knowing he is with us in all that we do.

The journey of life is a wonderful thing and it is even more wonderful when we place at the heart of it Christ's call to 'follow me'. For each of us, that call will mean different things, and that is the exciting thing – it is a unique and individual call to each of our lives. We don't often like surprises in life, unless they are the best kind, but surprised by Christ's call, and surprised by God's love for you and me, let us open our hearts and minds beyond the ordinary, and step forward in faith.

Time to reflect

- on when we felt the call of faith
- on where Christ is calling us now
- on the things we need to leave behind
- on the things we need to hold onto.

LIFE

2

Do not worry

Luke 12.22–31

If we could be given a pound for every time we have worried about something that has not then happened, most of us would be quite a bit richer than we are! It is easy to worry about anything from household bills, to the state of the world, to uncertainty in employment, to family frictions. The list could be endless! It is very difficult for a day to pass without some sort of worry entering our minds.

Into our minds then come these words of utter sense: 'Who of you by worrying can add a single hour to his life?' It's so obvious, it's so right, it's so true, but yet it's so difficult not to do it! Why did Jesus have to speak such sense? We prefer to worry away to ourselves, thank you very much!

These words of Jesus follow the parable of the Rich Fool, where treasures were stored up on earth rather than in heaven, and so the teaching of Jesus about priorities continues to his disciples in these words about worrying about tomorrow.

Life in Jesus' time was somewhat more precarious than our own existence in many ways, and so his words must have jarred with his hearers to a certain extent. They and we might want to say to Jesus, 'Well it's OK for you, you're the Son of God, but it's not quite so straightforward for us!'

However, Jesus was right about the futility of worrying, for it detracts rather than adds to life, and he was keen to help his followers, both then and now, to see the fuller life he was offering. That fullness of life is one that is founded on higher things than material wealth and possessions, and even more basic than daily bread. It is a life founded on faith, where God's provision is central to the life of the soul.

Jesus knows well that, despite his words, we will continue to worry about tomorrow, for he knows us better than we know ourselves. His words, though, stand as a marker to us in our lives of faith, about putting our trust in the right things, and placing our reliance on God. We have nothing to gain by worrying, and we have much to gain by trusting in God's way. Daily life is a blessing and should be seen as such, with Christ's teaching there to nudge fretful minds into gear when fear takes over.

Time to reflect

- on what makes us worry
- on Jesus' words of sense
- on what our priorities are
- on how we can live each day in fullness.

LIFE

3

Calm in the storm

Mark 4.35–41

None of us like circumstances that are outside our control. You only have to see how tempers fray at an airport when there are delays to flights and holidays are cancelled, to know how much we like order and predictability in our lives.

In recent years, there have been many natural events which have brought chaos and devastation to people's everyday existence. From floods and earthquakes, to drought and hurricane, the natural world is a force to be reckoned with, and things can change dramatically in a matter of seconds.

Jesus and his disciples found things changed rather quickly that day they sailed out on Lake Galilee when a storm got up. Jesus was exhausted from tending to the crowds that followed him and was lying peacefully asleep, apparently unaware of the fear and chaos that was unfolding around him. His disciples feared for their lives and were indignant that Jesus was doing nothing to help them.

Waking Jesus was the best thing they could do, for he was able to calm the storm, and silence their complaint, and presumably he was able then to go back to sleep, leaving the others to wonder about the power he held.

Of course, Jesus was quick to question their faith, as if to say, did they not trust that they would be OK with him beside them?

Perhaps we might have reacted in the same way as the disciples did. Presumably we are no different from them in our fears.

The fact that the storm arose, even though Jesus was with them in the boat, is a reminder to us that though we live our lives in faith, we are not immune to the storms of life which can swell up at any moment. We truly live a blessed life if we are never thrown about by the storms of life with their unexpected twists and turns.

Like the disciples with Jesus in the boat, we are challenged to live our lives trusting that while we have Christ with us, the storms may shake us, but they will not overwhelm us. In Christ we have one who is able to calm troubled hearts and minds amid the storm, and we have the comfort of knowing that we do not face anything in life alone.

Time to reflect

- on what shakes us in life
- on whether our faith is rooted in Christ
- on what storms we are facing now
- on trusting in the calming presence of God.

LIFE

4

The narrow way

Matthew 7.13-14

Driving in America is quite a different experience from driving in the UK. Super highways are everywhere, where huge numbers of traffic lanes, much wider than in the UK, converge around towns and cities. Drivers can happily sit with their automatic cars under cruise control as the fairly straight lanes take them to their destination. Add to that the comparatively cheap price of petrol, and it's no wonder there aren't many people keen to give up their cars for the sake of the environment.

It must be quite a culture shock to drive in Britain after the States, though, with our manual cars and our narrow winding roads with their ups and downs. The highways and routes of America are a much easier drive.

Life, similarly, is full of different roads for us to choose from. Some will be straight and wide, and others narrow and winding with some mountains and valleys in between. If we had the choice always within our control, than the easier option would be our preference no doubt. But life is never as straightforward as looking at a map and plotting your route. Things happen along the way that change how the journey of life unfolds.

So, too, in our journey of faith there are paths to choose from. Jesus talked about the narrow gate, and the narrow path leading to life, but said how many choose the wide road of destruction instead. It's a fairly easy thing for us to understand, for we all have the tendency to choose the easy way and to follow what the majority do.

Jesus was giving us guidance for life though, by asking us to take the different way – his way – for, in the narrow path, life would be found. In everyday situations and circumstances, we are encouraged to take the right path, even if it isn't the easiest one and, if we do so in faith, we will find our lives the fuller for that.

Each day brings different choices for us all as we walk along life's path, and it is good to keep that image of the narrow and wide gates at the forefront of our minds. Only a few will find the narrow way, says Jesus, but let us commit ourselves to being among them.

Time to reflect

- on where we take the easy path in life
- on times when the journey has been hard
- on times when we have been led in a surprising direction
- on what Jesus' words might mean for our daily choices.

KINGDOM

I

A place of welcome

Luke 23.32–43

If you could choose, how would you like your life to end and how would you like to be remembered? It's perhaps a morbid thought but, of course, one of the realities of life is that one day we will all die!

Most people would ideally like to live a happy and healthy life and one where years are numerous – to live to a ripe old age! Of course, most people would also like to come to life's end peacefully, and the often-voiced ideal is to die in one's sleep and at home.

How would you like to be remembered? As someone who made a difference to others? As a good friend and neighbour? As someone who 'did it my way'? Perhaps we might also like to be remembered for our faith.

Imagine for a moment if Jesus had been asked these questions about how he would want his life to end and how he would like to be remembered. Do you think his answers might have been terribly different from our own? It is hard to imagine that Jesus would have chosen to die in pain on a cross with two criminals for company.

And yet, perhaps it is in that stark image of three crosses, Jesus and the two robbers crucified together, that we can glimpse something of the kingdom that Christ preached.

In all his parables and teaching, Jesus revealed to his disciples and to each of us the way of God, and powerfully in his actions he turns those words into an example for each of us to follow. And even when the circumstances were taken outside his control, condemned to death by Pilate, and crucified outside the city walls, Jesus gives us a picture of what God's kingdom is about in reality.

While one of the criminals beside him continued to hurl abuse, the other realised that Jesus had done no wrong and was moved by his innocent suffering. 'Jesus, remember me, when you come into your kingdom,' he said.

In his response, Jesus gives a greater glimpse of that kingdom than he perhaps realised. Welcoming the man into God's presence, he said, 'Today you will be with me in paradise.'

We may or may not have committed crimes in our lives, but we have certainly all sinned and need to find that same love, acceptance and forgiveness. God's kingdom is something for us all to work towards, and it is a place where in faith we know we will find a welcome.

Time to reflect

- on the stretched-out arms of Christ for all
- on where we need forgiveness in our lives
- on the greatness of Christ's sacrifice
- on the kingdom we work for.

KINGDOM

2

A treasure of value

Matthew 13.44–6

There are some things we treasure in life more than others. If your home was on fire and you had the time to choose three things to take with you, what might they be? Presumably your first thought might be family members if they are in the home with you, but then it might come down to choices of personal mementos, computer files, photographs or jewellery. If you cannot think of three things that would matter all that much to you, then therein lies a parable about possessions!

Is there anything you desire so much that you would give up everything for it? That is a hard question to answer. Some have been known to sacrifice family and friends for the love of an individual. Others have given up honesty and respect for the gain of money. Life can be full of difficult choices.

But what of the kingdom of God? Is that something you consider to be of value? It is hard to grasp a concept that is not concrete in nature, but the parables of the Pearl and the Treasure teach us that the kingdom of heaven is of the greatest value and above all else.

Jesus talked often of God's kingdom and how his followers were to strive to be part of that kingdom in the future, but also to work towards that kingdom in the present. Jesus was clear that life was not to be lived with only a heavenly focus but, by his own example, he showed how life was to be lived bringing God's kingdom into the lives of others, through his love, teaching and healing.

The kingdom of heaven is one where salvation is to be found; a treasure of great price, but it is not found by ignoring the present reality. Jesus' good news for the poor and oppressed, and his radical teaching about living in love and service, needs to be lived out in word and action among his people today. It is not just in the future that salvation is found, but it is found in the present, bringing fullness of life to those who are oppressed and down trodden.

The kingdom of heaven is a great treasure to value, but our challenge is to bring that kingdom to earth in the way we live our lives of faith.

Time to reflect

- on what we value highly in life
- on what God's kingdom means to us
- on having our priorities right
- on striving for God's kingdom now.

KINGDOM

3

Without measure

Luke 21.1–4

'It's the thought that counts!' How often have we heard that said? But do we really believe it? Would you be offended if someone didn't give you a gift at your birthday, but reminded you it was the thought that counted? You might smile and agree, but feel inwardly upset. We all like to feel we are worth something. Equally if we are the one buying the gift, we like to put some thought into what to purchase, and we like to know that thought has been appreciated.

Have you ever wished you had more to give? That money would allow you to be more generous? I am sure the widow in the temple wished she had more to give than two small coins. Imagine how embarrassed she must have felt when the rich people were putting significant amounts into the treasury, and her two coins wouldn't even be enough to create a jingle.

Would we have been as brave as she, and given what little we had, or might we have considered that it was better to give nothing? There is little doubt that the rich people would have sneered at her meagre offering and thought it derisory of the God they worshipped.

But Jesus saw just how much she gave, and Jesus knew she had given her all. The others were merely giving what they could afford, but with all her heart she was giving all that she had left, probably wondering where her next meal might come from, and giving just the same.

How do we give in our own lives? Do we give without measure, or in a measured way? We will all no doubt answer the latter, for we have responsibilities and demands that are placed upon us financially, and it is hard to give without counting the cost.

Jesus never chastised those who gave out of their wealth, but he made the offering of the widow into an example for us all to learn from. Her faith and devotion has meant that her story has been held up in history as a powerful example of God's kingdom, where all is valued when given with a right heart.

We might often feel that we have little to give in working for God's kingdom, but the example of the widow's offering teaches us to give whatever we can. It also teaches us that what might seem insignificant to us can be seen by God to be of much higher value. God's kingdom is one where our values are often turned on their head, and rightly so.

Time to reflect

- on where we hold back on our giving
- on how we can give more abundantly
- on how we might be an example for others
- on how God's kingdom challenges ours.

KINGDOM

4

All are equal

Matthew 20.1–16

We can probably all remember learning our times tables in school, can't we? Reciting them out loud so that we knew that 2×2=4. Perhaps things are taught a bit differently in school today, but the answer will still be the same: 2×2 will always = 4.

When it comes to maths the equals sign '=' is part of most equations. When it comes to thinking about equality in life, things are a bit more complicated. There are probably people around us, friends or family or colleagues, that we might consider ourselves equal to in terms of status or power. It is more of a stretch of the imagination for us to consider that we might be equal to the person living on the street, equal to the drug addict, or equal to the refugee.

Jesus' parable of the Workers in the Vineyard is a stark wake-up call to how God's kingdom is ordered. The workers hired at the beginning of the day receive no more money than those hired at the end of the day who have only done one hour's work. All are treated equally and indeed fairly, for they have been paid what was promised to them.

You can imagine the arguments among the workers. 'But I worked much longer than he did!' 'And I worked much harder than she did!' 'I deserve far more than them, surely!'

We may not like to admit it openly, but we each hold within ourselves the idea that we are better than some people. We may have made better choices at times in our lives than some people, but as a human being, are we of any greater value than another? Not in God's kingdom! For in God's kingdom all are equal; the first shall be last, and there will be rejoicing for each one, no matter who they are, when they are received into God's presence.

When we can understand that we are all equal in the sight of God, we find a different orientation in our lives in terms of openness, love and service. Are we without sin? Then let us cast the first stone. Jesus came to place his kingdom values at the heart of our lives of faith, that we might see with his eyes and act with his heart, to know that 2×2 will always = 4, and that no matter who we are, God will love and accept us equally.

Time to reflect

- on where we hold attitudes of prejudice
- on whether we think the parable is fair
- on who is our equal
- on whether we deserve God's love any more than another.

CHALLENGE

I

Common sense

Mark 2.23–7

'You've just got no common sense!' I wonder how many times we have heard that sentiment addressed in our direction? Sometimes in jest no doubt, and sometimes in all seriousness. By the very nature of the word 'common', common sense is something which should be present in all of us, but at times is sadly lacking.

Consider the times when you know you have been foolish and felt more than a bit stupid. It happens to all of us! But what also normally happens, or what also hopefully happens, is that we each learn from our mistakes and try not to let the same faults repeat themselves.

Consider then, how frustrated Jesus must have found himself becoming, when not just surrounded by his own disciples who didn't often manage to grasp the full picture, but when also being challenged on a regular basis by the Pharisees, the religious leaders, who were very self assured in their knowledge of the Scriptures and in what God's teaching said.

It's a shame they didn't have the common sense to see Jesus for what he was, God's own Son, and to learn from him, rather than to challenge and question him, to try and find fault with him so that they might discredit him as a heretic.

The challenge to Jesus about his disciples picking heads of corn from the field on the Sabbath has to be considered as one of the pettiest examples of their cause. Can that really be considered work? But of course, Jesus, himself fully knowledgeable in the Scriptures, is able to counter their challenge with his own example from Scripture, and with his common-sense response, 'The Sabbath was made for man, and not man for the Sabbath. So the Son of Man is Lord even of the Sabbath.'

We can each learn from this story, about the pettiness of human nature and the common-sense approach of Jesus which we are called to follow. Equally, we are also reminded that knowledge of the Scriptures is a helpful thing, both for our own lives of faith, but also in responding to the questions that others might throw in our direction. There are many who would like to discredit the Christian faith and challenge it at every opportunity, but if we live with faith and with common sense, we can be confident that like Christ we can readily respond to that challenge.

Time to reflect

- on the times we act with pettiness like the Pharisees
- on the lessons we can learn from Christ's response
- on how to respond to the challenges that confront our faith
- on our need of God's wisdom.

CHALLENGE

2

Recognising our faults

Luke 6.37–42

There are some wonderful sayings in the English language that can say something challenging but also can be said with a twinkle in the eye. 'That will be the pot calling the kettle black!' is one such phrase. A direct, yet jovial way of telling someone they are being somewhat hypocritical. No doubt that is something we are all guilty of at various times.

It is a fascinating trait of human nature that we have the ability to see the faults of others with acute attention to detail while we can blithely pretend that we do not have the same fault in ourselves. A classic example would be gossiping about someone because they are known to be a gossip, without realising that in doing so, we are doing the same!

Jesus was pretty direct in his challenge to his followers about not judging others, and not criticising another's faults, without first of all addressing our own faults. He doesn't use some jovial turn of phrase, but just comes out with some pretty straight-talking advice about how to live our lives.

Here we are taught not to judge or condemn, and to be giving and forgiving. We are also bluntly reminded that we should not be hypocritical and see the speck in another's eye, without removing the plank in our own. It's a wonderful turn of phrase, and one to be remembered.

We all desire to be treated well in life and be given due respect and attention. How, then, can we fail to do the same for our neighbours in the world? Jesus reminds us that the measure we give will be the measure that we are given, and there are strong parallels with his command to treat others as you would want to be treated yourself.

Each of us is challenged to see the faults that lie within ourselves, and with God's help to work towards improving them. There is nothing wrong with challenging other people in God's name where something is wrong or unjust, but we must make sure we are above the same criticism ourselves, or we will simply be seen as a 'pot calling a kettle black' and our words will lose all meaning.

Time to reflect

- on our readiness to criticise others
- on where our own faults lie
- on our need for God's help to change
- on when we can justly criticise.

CHALLENGE

3

A step too far?

John 6.60–9

Have you ever got involved in something you wish you hadn't? It needn't be something sinister, just something where you have found yourself more deeply involved than first planned, and at some point you've had to pull back. It might even be that this has happened to you in the church. There is a joke that once you volunteer to do something on a temporary basis in the church, you'll end up doing it for years!

Sometimes we are full of enthusiasm when we become part of something, and so we readily offer to take on responsibility and become further involved, but sometimes things happen to make us reconsider. It may be that the commitment is just too draining on our time, or there are some personality clashes, or it's all just proving to be too much effort.

Jesus had many disciples outside of the twelve chosen we normally think of. There were many people who listened to him and saw him in action, and then decided to follow too. That was until the teaching became too challenging and some of them reconsidered their position.

Jesus had been teaching his followers and alluding to his death, talking of his body becoming bread and speaking of a time when they would drink his blood, and some of the disciples were clearly disgusted by the idea. This was just a step too far. There were rumbling voices of discontent and as a result a number of his followers decided to desert him, but the chosen twelve remained faithful.

We don't often hear about people choosing to desert Jesus in this way, for we are more used to hearing about people joining his following. It is a stark reminder to us that the decision we make to follow Christ is not an easy one, and his teaching will continue to be challenging as we live our lives in faith.

With the hindsight we have, we can understand what Jesus was trying to teach his followers, and that the path that lay ahead would not be smooth and easy. So too, as we follow Christ today, we also understand that challenges to our faith arise on a regular basis.

For each of us, we are asked to be faithful, and recognise that Jesus is the one with the words of eternal life. We are also challenged to draw closer to God and involve ourselves more deeply in that relationship and, far from finding that we have got in too deep, we will find we have arrived in a place of blessing and promise.

Time to reflect

- on how challenging we find Jesus' teaching
- on times we have found having faith hard
- on how we think we might have reacted ourselves to this teaching
- on what we can learn from those who remained true to Jesus.

CHALLENGE

4

Living with questions

John 3.1–8

Have you ever lain awake at night wondering or worrying about something? There is something about the quietness and darkness of lying down to sleep that allows all those unanswered questions to come into our minds to hinder our sleep. Sometimes we can turn things over and over in our minds, feeling like we are getting nowhere, and we might lose a few hours' sleep without getting any further forward. Sometimes it's better just to get up and deal with things if we can.

It's perhaps a sympathetic view to have of Nicodemus, who came to Jesus at night, but maybe he was mulling over in his mind what he had heard Jesus say and what he had seen him do and, rather than be kept awake all night, he decided to go and see Jesus and ask him. Others will say that Nicodemus came to Jesus by night because he was afraid of being found out, but even if so, it is clear that Nicodemus had questions burning in his mind.

Nicodemus probably got more than he bargained for though, when Jesus told him that to see the kingdom of God, he would have to be born again. Clearly Nicodemus struggled with the very practicalities of that concept, and thought Jesus was speaking literally!

These were very challenging words of Jesus to Nicodemus, and they remain very challenging to us today. To be born again means having a new spiritual birth, so that one is transformed from the old into the new by the Spirit of God.

Sadly the call to be born again has often been hijacked by certain groups within the Christian Church to become a threatening question rather than an open invitation of God. Many people will feel that they have had a gradual coming to faith in their lives, rather than some immediate conversion experience, and this should never be underestimated. If we look at the example of the first disciples, they too had a very gradual awakening to Christ's teaching and influence in their lives.

Each of us, like Nicodemus, is invited to ask the questions we have of God, and to invite God's Spirit to live and breathe within us, guiding and guarding our lives. It is that same Spirit that can bring us the comfort and peace that we might need in the still watches of the night, as we wrestle with issues of life and faith. It is that same Spirit who wakes with us each day and goes before us to guide our way.

Time to reflect

- on what keeps us awake at night
- on the questions of faith we have
- on how we sense God's Spirit in our lives
- on how we might live as born-again people.

LIGHT

I

Seeing clearly

John 1.1–9

Have you ever had that experience of waking up and wondering where you are? Perhaps you've been on holiday somewhere or visiting friends, but as you come to in the morning, you are confused by your surroundings just for a moment or two, until you open your eyes to focus, and allow the light to reveal the blurred objects around you so that you remember where you are. Then it all makes sense!

There's something of that early confusion and gradual dawning of light found in the opening words of John's Gospel – a light shining in the darkness, but where the darkness has not understood it.

People were looking for light in the time of Christ. Their lives were dark in many ways, living a hard life, often without hope, and having to contend with disease and poverty, and a fair amount of corruption too. They were looking for someone to come and show them the way, and they welcomed John the Baptist and his message of repentance, but more importantly his promise about the one coming after him, whose light would bring life.

Light is a contagious sort of thing. You see people become brighter and cheerier on a sunny day as light floods onto their faces, warming their bodies and making folk smile, even when they don't realise it. Light brings a certain positivity to life that is hard to escape, and it brings welcome refreshment.

People continue to live in the darkness today, trodden down by daily life, and unable sometimes to see that light of Christ which is equally contagious, refreshing and life giving. Sometimes the darkness around can make the light distorted and confusing, and make it hard to find one's bearings.

Just as it takes a little time to orientate oneself to the light in the morning, so people often need a little help to orientate themselves towards the light of Christ – someone to show them the way, and help them navigate through a dimly lit room.

As Christ shines his light into our lives of faith, so he also asks us to continue to be light to his world and to his people, radiating something of his love and care to those who so desperately need to find him. Like John the Baptist, we are asked to point the way to the one who is the source of all things.

Time to reflect

- on how we feel when light shines upon us
- on the areas of our lives that are dark
- on how we can share the light of Christ
- on how that light is for all people.

LIGHT

2

Light and dark

Genesis 1.1–5

There is something very powerful in watching the sun rise, flooding the earth with its light. There is something equally powerful in watching the sun set and darkness descend. It is also a powerful thought to realise that as darkness descends where we are in the world, light is dawning elsewhere, and when light is dawning where we are, darkness is descending somewhere else. Truly we live in a remarkable world.

From the origins of human life people have observed the same routine of light and dark, the rising and setting of the sun, and so, as creation is explained in the story we find in Genesis, we begin with such a powerful separation of light and darkness, on the first day.

Despite the passage of the centuries, and the explorations of science, Genesis still gives us a powerful understanding of God's work in creation, and in the formation of the world and its people as we know them. Truly the earth was a formless void in its infancy, and we know that the light of the sun allowed all sorts of evolution to take place on land and in sea.

The separation of the light and dark is a powerful metaphor in the Christian faith, and quite rightly we find it right at the beginning of the story of faith, where God is working out his purpose in bringing light and life to all humanity. It is comforting to know that our ancestors of faith before us felt the warmth of the same sun on their backs and knew that God was active in their world.

From those early words in Genesis, light is seen as good, and darkness is seen as something less good. That is something we can still understand today. It is in darkness that most crimes are committed, and when people are ill or struggling, their lives are described as dark. We see the light as something positive in comparison, and something that brings life, just as is depicted in Genesis.

As part of creation, there is a need in all of us to allow God to separate the light and dark in our own lives, and to allow something of good to be created. We all have our own personal places of void and emptiness, and God offers to flood those parts of life with his light.

Each day that the sun rises and sets is a new day, a new day with God, and we are invited to let his light fill and guide our lives as we become a new creation.

Time to reflect

- on where we need light in our lives
- on where there is still darkness in the world
- on the gift of each new day
- on what it is to be a new creation.

LIGHT

3

Let your light shine

Matthew 5.14–16

Unless you work in publicity, advertising or PR, you will probably not be very keen to shout about your skills and talents. Even if you do work in these areas, you will no doubt be happier promoting the skills and talents of someone else, or of a particular product, than you would be about talking about yourself.

The popularity of the TV series *The Apprentice* has seen some very confident people come and go, and part of its appeal to the viewer is surely to see people taken down a peg or two from their extreme confidence in their abilities. Many are able to 'talk the talk' but not 'walk the walk' and they are not able to live up to what they claim to be.

When Jesus said that 'you are the light of the world', as part of his Sermon on the Mount, there must have been some people thinking that they had misheard. Surely he must have meant he was the light of the world! But no, you are the light of the world.

How can we be the light of the world? How can individuals like us, without bags of confidence, be so important to the world? How can people who sometimes struggle with the demands of daily life, be like a light to others? Surely Jesus is wonderfully mistaken in our abilities!

That might be true if we were simply left to our own devices but, throughout his Sermon, Jesus is encouraging an understanding of, and a reliance on, God and explaining how God works through people, just as God is working through him. If God is light, then by being in relationship with God that light is able to flow through us, so we might be an example for others to follow.

It is very easy for us to talk down our importance as individuals, but Jesus reminds us that you do not hide a light, but put it on a stand, so that it might give light to others. As we hold onto the faith we have and share in Christ, we are asked to step out confidently in his name, allowing the light he has brought into our lives to spread to others.

Let us not be guilty of hiding what we have been blessed to receive. Let us rise to the challenge of being a light to the world.

Time to reflect

- on where we lack confidence
- on the confidence we can gain through Christ
- on how we might make our light shine
- on those whose example we might follow.

LIGHT

4

New sight

John 9.1-7

For the majority of us who are blessed with our sight in life, one of our greatest fears is to lose that ability to see. Never again to be able to look at the beauty of the world around us, the changing of the seasons, the budding of a flower, the beauty of a sunset; it is a hard thing to imagine. Advances in medical science have led to great improvements in preserving and restoring sight, but there are limits of course.

Would it be better to have been born blind, than to be born with sight only to lose it? It is a difficult question to answer. The man in the story from John's Gospel had been born blind and had never seen the world around him, nor his own family. Added to that was the belief that his condition was something to do with his sin, or the sin of his parents. However, Jesus was quick to clear up that misunderstanding when his disciples asked.

Jesus chose to bring healing to the man to help his disciples understand the man's condition – but also to help them understand his power and purpose. In bringing sight to the blind man, he revealed that he was the light of the world, and brought new light, in every way, into that man's life.

In doing so he was teaching his followers that he was able to bring that same light into the lives of all who would believe in him that they might see, and see in a new way.

In a sense, each of us is blind to the world in some ways. We choose often to see the things we want to see and ignore the things we want to ignore. If we truly allow Jesus' light to shine in and through our lives, then he will reveal to us a different way of looking at things.

Jesus has the power and the purpose to help us look at things in a new and transforming way. He has the power to make us see things with his eyes, that we might see life with all its shame and injustice. He has the purpose to help us look at things in a new and transforming way, so that we might continue being his light in the world.

Jesus was clear that he was to be light as long as he was in the world, but he said that night was coming. He was aware of his own ministry being a short one, and of the need for his followers to continue his saving work. May we be open to his gift of light and new sight, that we might live our lives for him, shedding light and life through our words and actions.

Time to reflect

- on the gift of sight
- on how we can see things in a new way
- on how we can challenge prejudice
- on the call to continue to shed Christ's light.

GROUP PRAYER RESPONSES

(Suitable for photocopying or printing out)

During our worship there will be:

Music: Listen to the words being sung and make them your words, or let the music guide your thoughts.

Stillness: Use the stillness to talk to God, to rest in God's presence, and to think on your life and faith.

Prayer: Let the words spoken become your prayer. It may help to repeat the words into yourself.

Reading: Listen to God's words and let them reach you. Try to hear the words for the first time and note your reaction.

Reflection: What might God be saying to you today? What can you learn from God?

TIMING

DRAWING NEAR

Time never stands still
But our God is eternal

Yesterday, today and tomorrow
God is unchanging

Here and now, in this precious time
May we meet with God

Worshipping together

CLOSING RESPONSES

All time is in God's hands
Lord, we have met with you this day/night

Into your hands we commit our lives
Bless us, O Lord God of life

Send us out in your name
Go with us now, we pray.

BLESSING

**May God bless, preserve and keep us, now and for evermore.
Amen**

UNITY

DRAWING NEAR

Where two or three are gathered
God is there

As we gather this day/night
God is here

Here and now and always
God is with us

Worshipping together

CLOSING RESPONSES

Make us one, Lord, in your love
Make us one, Lord, in your name

May your life be known in our lives
May your love shine through us

BLESSING

**May the blessing of the one, and the blessing of the three,
entwine together thee and me. Amen**

PROVIDENCE

DRAWING NEAR

In the journey of life
God makes known a path

Through rough and smooth, twist and turn
God is our guiding strength

Through the adventure that is faith
Our trust is in God

Worshipping together

CLOSING RESPONSES

Our God has shown us the Way
Let us walk forward in faith

Our God has revealed to us the Truth
Let us live in truth each day

Our God has blessed us with Life
Let us live our lives for God

BLESSING

May God grant his blessing to each and to all, both now and for evermore. Amen

CREATION

DRAWING NEAR

Through sunshine, cloud and rain
God blesses the earth

Amid earth's myriad of colours
God's glory is seen

As part of God's creation
We know our Creator is near

Worshipping together

CLOSING RESPONSES

From the earth we came
We belong to God

To the earth we will return
We belong to God

Let us go to care for the earth and its people
For we belong to God

BLESSING

May God add his blessing to his creation, through us, his creation. In Christ's name. Amen

GROWTH

DRAWING NEAR

As new buds burst forth in Springtime
May our love for God blossom

Where beauty and colour enrich the earth
May our lives be a fragrant offering

As a seed sown awaits its potential
May we grow each day in God

Worshipping together

CLOSING RESPONSES

Rooted in God
Let us go forward in faith

Nourished in the Lord
Let us go in his strength

Fed by his Word
Let us live to his glory

BLESSING

May the blessing of God guard, support and sustain us, each and every day. Amen

SERVICE

DRAWING NEAR

Call to us now, Lord
That we may hear your voice

Come to us now, Lord
That we might seek your way

Meet with us now, Lord
That we might praise your name

Worshipping together

CLOSING RESPONSES

Our God calls us to serve
May we not seek to be served

Through Christ we see the way
May we follow in faith

As Jesus pointed to the Father
Let all glory be to God alone

BLESSING

May the blessing of the God of Life, the Christ of Love and the Spirit of Peace be with us all. Amen

JUSTICE

DRAWING NEAR

The Lord is just and merciful
His compassion is unending

He is perfect beyond compare
His faithfulness is never exhausted

He is higher than the heavens, yet present with us now
Let us draw near to God

Worshipping together

CLOSING RESPONSES

A blameless life, given for us
Let your life be lived in ours

A wondrous love, gifted to us
Let your love be seen in us

A life of justice, lived in truth
Let justice reign in our hearts

BLESSING

**May grace, mercy and peace from God the Father, Spirit and Son
guide our lives and our living, this and every day. Amen**

LOVE

DRAWING NEAR

Love is greater than all things
Our God is love

His love is arms stretched out upon a cross
Our God is love

Such love calls us to humble service
Let us love God with heart, mind, soul and strength

Worshipping together

CLOSING RESPONSES

God is love
We go to live in the love of God

God is life
We go to live in fullness of life

God is living
We go to spread the good news

BLESSING

**May Christ's blessing go before and behind us, and be known
through us day by day. Amen**

LIFE

DRAWING NEAR

God calls us to new life in him
Every day is new with God

God calls us to life in all its fullness
May the Spirit fill our lives

Life in God is life everlasting
May our lives be filled with praise

Worshipping together

CLOSING RESPONSES

Hope is a gift from God
Let us go with hope in our hearts

Peace is a gift from God
Let us share the peace of Christ

Joy is a gift from God
Let the joy of Christ fill our lives

BLESSING

**May the blessing of God be with us, and with all God's people,
now and always. Amen**

KINGDOM

DRAWING NEAR

Your kingdom come, Lord
Your will be done

Let your kingdom be established
Let it be established in me

Your kingdom come, Lord
Let it begin with me

Worshipping together

CLOSING RESPONSES

The kingdom of God is here
It is here in me

The kingdom of God is now
Let it live in me

Your will be done, living God
On earth as it is in heaven. Amen

BLESSING

May God bless us as we walk forward in faith, living in his truth, and sharing in his work. Amen

CHALLENGE

DRAWING NEAR

From the security of our lives
We come to the sanctuary of God

Amid the world's noises and demands
We come to the peace of God

As we gather together in Christ's name
God, meet us here, we pray

Worshipping together

CLOSING RESPONSES

God goes before us
To show us the way

God goes behind us
Let us not stray

God goes with us
Bless us, we pray

BLESSING

May God grant his blessing to us as we go forward, keeping alive the faith, day by day. Amen

LIGHT

Out of the darkness and the void
Your light began to shine

Into the dark places of our lives
Shine your light, Lord

Into the dark corners of this world
Let us shine for you

Worshipping together

CLOSING RESPONSES

Light has come into the world
And the darkness cannot hide it

Light has come in Christ our Lord
And the earth has seen his glory

Light has come into our lives
And we have been changed

BLESSING

**May the light of Christ bring blessing to us and all God's people,
both now and for evermore. Amen**